T0208954

The Spirit In Nature

A Scientific History of the Universe From a Spiritual Perspective

Kim Richard Wallace, M.ED

BALBOA.PRESS

A DIVISION OF HAY HOUSE

Balboa Press books may be ordered through booksellers or by contacting:

Balboa Press
A Division of Hay House
1663 Liberty Drive
Bloomington, IN 47403
www.balboapress.com
1 (877) 407-4847

Because of the dynamic nature of the Internet, any web addresses or
links contained in this book may have changed since publication and may
no longer be valid. The views expressed in this work are solely those
of the author and do not necessarily reflect the views of the publisher,
and the publisher hereby disclaims any responsibility for them.

The author of this book does not dispense medical advice or prescribe
the use of any technique as a form of treatment for physical, emotional,
or medical problems without the advice of a physician, either directly
or indirectly. The intent of the author is only to offer information
of a general nature to help you in your quest for emotional and
spiritual well-being. In the event you use any of the information in
this book for yourself, which is your constitutional right, the author
and the publisher assume no responsibility for your actions.

Any people depicted in stock imagery provided by Getty Images are
models, and such images are being used for illustrative purposes only.
Certain stock imagery © Getty Images.

Print information available on the last page.

ISBN: 978-1-9822-3949-7 (sc)
ISBN: 978-1-9822-3950-3 (e)

Balboa Press rev. date: 01/16/2020

CONTENTS

INTRODUCTION

THE SPIRIT IN NATURE

This is a collection of essays, which for the most part is an attempt to bridge the gap between a scientific perspective and a spiritual one. A lot of this unfortunate distance seems to derive from the antagonism that the scientific community has with the anti-evolution/Old Testament orientation of the religious fundamentalists. I'm not sure that this gap can ever be overcome if a person is not willing to look squarely and objectively at the facts at hand because of previously held beliefs. This inability is an undeniable aspect of human nature, proven by a multitude of psychological studies and our own personal experiences.

There are, as we all know, a fairly large number of people that have decided to take the Bible literally. This can be compared to taking a poem or the lyrics to a song literally (not that they have the same level of significance). You can try to do it, but you have no way of knowing if "your" literal interpretation is the correct one. The world is full of religious sects that have been founded by men and women who have made what they believe to be the correct, inspired interpretation of religious texts.

For instance, which one of the hundreds of Protestant sects in western culture is correctly conveying the truth, as the authors of the texts had originally presented it? General effects like the language and the social and cultural context of the time in which the original text was created should always be taken into consideration, along with what was common knowledge, or the lack of it, at the time when it was written. In particular, what was the general level of scientific knowledge that was available to the common men and women of the time, if any?

Science as we know it was not even invented (except with a small group of Greeks) at the time most of the early Biblical texts were created. Also, at the time the manuscripts were produced hardly anyone could read, except a select few, and even for the literate, there was a lack of books available. Things considered truths, or any other abstract ideas, were conveyed in a metaphorical or allegorical way, which is still common today. Most of us aren't interested in this type of in-depth evaluation of the scriptures, unless of course, we're scholars specializing in such things. Nevertheless they should be taken into consideration.

Getting back to the lyrics of songs by way of an analogy, I think most of us have seen or read interviews with people who have written a song or poem, and when they were asked what their meaning had been when they originally wrote it, it ends up being considerably and surprisingly different from what we might have assumed. The Bible could be seen in that way, at least to some extent.

The Bible is a compilation of books written by different authors at different times and places, and most of the books, if not all, have gone through multiple translations (Hebrew, Aramaic, Greek, Latin and Old English to Modern English, to name a few). Also, we don't always realize that the books which were selected to be in the Bible had originally been passed around individually and copied for that purpose, and were not compiled into one book, the text that is in common usage today, until hundreds of years later. There were a number of books that could have been included which were left out, as we are now discovering. So the question arises, who was at the table making the decisions and why were certain books omitted? It is a complicated, interesting story that this book really can't address but only touch upon.

The reason that there are four gospels instead of three, for instance, is that there are four directions, and the compilers of the books that became the New Testament decided there should be the same number of books as directions. That is why John's gospel has a different, more philosophical Greek orientation, as opposed to the three synoptic gospels that are derived from a common source more Jewish in nature. We also know that words change their meaning over time and can be mistranslated. A single word like faith, for instance, which has profound theological implications, can change depending on how it is interpreted or how it has been translated.

It is plain to see if one believes that the interpretation given by an institution or an esteemed individual is the correct one, that this can lead to all sorts of tragic consequences if that interpretation is taken as the infallible truth and others are forced to believe it as such. Some of those tragedies are obvious, such as the perpetrating of unspeakable horrors which some people feel are justified, in the name of a merciful God, no less. We are often faced with this aspect of religion, as it plays out in history books and the daily news. However, we will be putting all that aside, because this book is not about correlating religion per se with science; it is about the evidence put forth by science supporting the high probability that the Universe is a spiritual manifestation that is not separate from Spirit, but is an expression of Spirit, with Spirit being present in every aspect of it.

Unfortunately, with our busy lives, we usually have neither the time, nor energy to investigate what science has to say about the possibility of an underlying spiritual dynamic in the unfolding of the Universe, or we have not given a hard look at how the life and consciousness found within the Universe came about. This book is an attempt to help those people who wonder if science has ruled out the possibility of the existence of God, as many have argued.

We can find many people among our friends and acquaintances who wonder if they are being foolish or naive to think there is an underlying spiritual aspect to life because of something they have read or heard that seems to rule out that possibility. The premise of this collection of essays is that looking at the scientific evidence objectively, with an open mind, can lead us to feel differently.

God can be conceptualized as being personal or impersonal. These essays will explore, by and large, what would generally be considered the impersonal aspects of Spirit as it pertains to the Universe at large and its unfolding.

We, by definition, should develop our own personal orientation towards how we conceptualize Spirit in any way that resonates with us as individuals.

From my perspective, the personal aspect of God is manifest in us all. We are embedded in and participating in that which we call God, except that we don't see and feel it that way. Some people seem to have realized this fact and present their varied experiences of it in their personal testimonies, but most of us haven't had that experience, or if we have had it, it was fleeting. I believe that God can be thought of as both infinite and finite at the same time: beyond the Universe and also in every particle of it.

As children growing up most of us inevitably become desensitized to the strangeness of it all. We didn't realize that there is absolutely no reason for any of this, the Universe and our lives in general, to have happened. Why would we? We were born into it and it was our reality. As we grew older, on reflection, we could perhaps have thought nothing should exist if we had a philosophical bent to our natures. But there was at that time no evidence one way or another. Cosmology has made great strides since then, and now there is firm evidence informing us of the Universe's nascent beginning.

In that not so distant past, many scientists liked to think of the Universe as eternal; that way no deep philosophical speculations were necessary about its origin. Even Einstein himself thought the Universe was eternal, until he was presented with overwhelming evidence that it was not.

In the Western world because of a few New and Old Testament quotes, along with our own personal experiences, we have developed the mentality that we are somehow separate and fundamentally different from the rest of the natural world. This is common enough in our culture, but I believe it is a perceptual and conceptual mistake. My basic contention is that if we are so inclined, we could see as I touched on earlier, the Universe as an expression of the Infinite Spirit. This is the central premise of this collection of essays.

Try to think of it this way: before the act of creation, the Infinite which was going to create the Universe at that particular moment, could not conceivably have found something outside of itself with which to create the Universe. It had to manifest "Itself" as the Universe. It is not philosophically or logically possible for it to have been any other way; nothing is outside of Infinity. So from that perspective, we are living and participating (co-creating) in that which we usually call God. This is obviously not an easy thing to appreciate or realize.

There is an old fable along these lines that goes something like this: there was a group of fish that had gotten together, and they were trying to understand what the ocean was. They talked it over and couldn't really figure it out. So one of the fish suggested that they put the question before an old wise fish that they had heard about. They managed to find the old fish and ask it to explain to them the ocean. The old wise fish told them the ocean was that in which they moved, lived, and had their being. It was all-pervasive and everything they experienced took place within it. They thanked the old fish for his time and swam away. After they had departed they got back together and talked it over and decided that they still didn't understand!

When people make the statement: "If there is a God, what created God?" they miss the point that causality (cause leading to an effect) as we think about it, is solely an aspect of this Universe and doesn't pertain to that which lies beyond it. Causality is only relevant when you are talking about something within the context of time and space. Causality needs time, space, and energy, and is meaningless without them. These three things, and they are things by the way, don't exist outside of the Universe. Time, space, and energy were all created together at the moment of creation and are limited to and only exist within the Universe, and when you use words like eternal and infinity which concern that which lies beyond the Universe, they are well beyond our capacities to understand or conceptualize. Our brains with their limited abilities to think about such things can only go so far.

From the perspective that will be presented in this book, Spirit at this very moment is actively conceptualizing and sustaining every particle, form, and force that the Universe contains. Underlying it all is consciousness, which must be an essential aspect of Spirit. What we are experiencing now is a very small part of that infinite consciousness in our isolated, accustomed, and limited way. We are never separate for a moment, and we can and, I believe, should, realize that fact more fully to our advantage. This seems odd and improbable to most of us, but we will see that this is the reality of our existence in all probability.

Again, the goal of the bulk of the essays contained in this work is to present the facts as they are being discovered by science, and to offer these facts as reasonable proof that this orientation and perspective is correct beyond a reasonable doubt. The Universe is an interesting story to be told; let us begin.

ONE

IN THE BEGINNING

Something extraordinary happened 13.8 billion or so years ago. Our universe came into existence. Before then there was nothing. Some physicists and cosmologists, because they don't like the idea of something from nothing, (who normally would?) say that our universe was a product of an eternal-infinite series of other universes with different laws and fundamental constants. This idea doesn't explain anything about why there are these adjustable things like laws and constants. Fundamental constants, by the way, are effects such as the sizes, charges, spins, and strengths of the particles along with their interactions, as well as the strengths of the fundamental forces found in Nature, such as gravity and the strong and weak nuclear forces intrinsic in atoms (there are well over 20 such parameters in play governing the Universe).

But whether there are other Universes or not we will never know, because any hypothesis about what went on before the act of creation can only be speculative. It is not possible for science to go past the point of creation, or even to the exact point of creation for that matter, those speculating can only offer informed guesses about possibilities, and as appealing as some of their ideas can be, there will never be any conclusive proof one way or the other. But what we do know is here we are, in a Universe that is remarkably well adjusted and incredibly fine-tuned that has allowed life to emerge within it.

Let's try to imagine the unimaginable for a moment: there is "nothing" at all and spontaneously there springs forth this thing that we now are experiencing called the Universe. Shockingly, it was so small to begin with that it would have been invisible even to the most powerful microscope available to us on the planet. It was that small. That seems to be ridiculous and impossible – right? But all the scientific evidence supports this improbable fact.

Immediately, this speck takes off and in an instant gets really huge (about the size of our galaxy it has been estimated - which is about 100 thousand light years across). Near the start of this rapid expansion that is now called inflation, let us press a hypothetical pause button. Let's stop this incredibly swift spreading out of this newly minted space and time for a moment, at the size of something that would fit comfortably in the palm of our hand, like an apple for instance, and take inventory. To start with, we have something that is almost infinitely hot; brilliantly hot to the point that the zeros after the one describing how hot it is, would go off the chart.

Surprisingly, there is a lot of hidden potential to be found in this little fluctuating but relatively uniform space-time fireball;

a tremendous amount of what we call information that is just starting to be revealed in a multitude of different ways. Let us briefly consider where all this information must have come from (information doesn't just spring into existence on its own, at least not in our experience). In the realm of science, the information found in any system, such as a cell or a Cadillac for that matter, always comes from the environment in which it arises (this is common sense if you think about it for a moment). For instance, all the biological information in our DNA comes from the long series of environments in which it evolved.

This fact is fairly obvious in the information being expressed in our everyday lives. We are generally aware on some level of all the ingenuity and creativity that went into the making of the devices we are quite often dealing with throughout the day. Now I think it should be asked, where did and does all the information found in the universe come from? I think we can say the logical answer would be from the environment, so to speak, that contains and is manifesting itself as the Universe. We will remember that it is logically inconsistent to imagine that whatever is manifesting this Universe found something outside of itself to create a Universe with.

Some would call that of which we are speaking, God (there is a lot of very heavy baggage with this word), the Infinite Spirit, the Source, or as many American Indians would say the Great Spirit. Take your pick or make up your own name for it if you like (I'm sure it won't mind). But what we are talking about is beyond anything we can possibly envision or conceptualize. We are talking about something that at this very moment is actively imagining, so to speak, and sustaining every particle, form and force that enables us to be here. It's also, I believe, the bedrock of the magic we experience as consciousness.

Now let's get back to that little ball of red-hot-energetic space-time. At this point in its existence the Universe has interacted with itself on a quantum level (sub-atomic) that we are still remarkably able to see to this day with the sophisticated satellites that have recently been put into orbit. Astonishingly, the images produced show the fluctuations that were going on back when the Universe was just trillionths of a second old.

There is a homogeneity found in this background radiation that has been imaged, and it is so uniform and similar in all directions that the early Universe had to have interacted with itself to achieve this effect. There is no other way, because to realize this effect, the interactions that are necessary to create it would have had to have happened at a rate well beyond the speed of light, and nothing in our Universe can do that. So unexpectedly, we get to see the radiant and homogeneous features of the infant Universe when it was no bigger than the period at the end of this sentence. This, by the way, is just one of the many accumulating confirmations of the early quantum-then-inflationary period in the history of the Universe - there are many more we will encounter.

I think at this point it would be nice to give a little tribute to the commitment and ingenuity of the thousands of scientists and technicians who have generated all the detailed knowledge we are going to explore in the upcoming essays (the perspective derived from this information is a gift). Their search for the truth, and how far we have come in understanding how all this came to be (the unfolding of the Universe leading to us) is an extraordinary achievement and should be more widely appreciated. Their efforts have been heroic in my opinion.

That being said, in the next essay we will start looking at the odd and unexpected things that started to emerge after the Universe had, for some unknown reason, started to slow down its incredibly rapid expansion and in the process had started to cool off, enabling some interesting things to occur.

TWO

SPACE, TIME AND ENERGY

Everything we hold near and dear has emerged from space-time and the energy contained in its fabric. What is this remarkable stuff that sprang into existence out of the Infinite, and what are some of its qualities? For instance, the particles that jumped into existence after the brief-initial-inflationary expansion of space had slowed and cooled somewhat, were a latent aspect of space, an excitation of fields that were and are embedded in space. Each particle, we now know, is an expression of a point in space, belonging to a field that corresponds to it, and space is absolutely loaded with these fields (who would have thought?). For example, an electron is a minuscule vortex, or perhaps something like a minute vibrating string like structure, as some physicists speculate, in the electron field that pervades the entire Universe.

We see these particles all around us in matter and light, and we perceive space as a blank nothingness, but all these particles are aspects of space and not separate from it in any way – they are space! To think of this in a two-dimensional way, imagine a large stiff bristle brush with a thin plastic sheet draped over it. You apply energy to the plastic membrane by pulling it tight and pushing it down on the brush. What you then would see are small dimples in the sheet where the bristles are pushed up against it. Particles are a little like those dimples, but with the big difference that the fields that are manifesting as particles are three-dimensionally pervasive in all of space; the particles being small points of concentrated energy capable of movement within those fields. A little like when you move your foot or hand under the covers to play with your cat or dog (skip this analogy if you don't have pets).

Time is also an aspect of space, and it is a peculiar thing to think about. Where mass or energy is strong, it slows and flows in a more restricted way than where the mass in space is inconsequential. Time flows slower at the base of a mountain, for instance, than at the top because of less gravitational force being found at the top of the mountain. The effect is negligible; you would need a sophisticated atomic clock to detect the difference.

I remember reading years ago that scientists, in order to prove this point, put an atomic clock on a supersonic jet and flew it around the world as swiftly as they could and it came back having slowed, ever so slightly, compared to the one that remained behind. Again this is because of the effect of the extra mass generated by the energy propelling the motion of the jet (energy equals mass). A jet in motion has more mass than a jet at rest, so the faster you go in a jet, the slower time goes compared to someone or something that is stationary. As an aside, many things used by us daily, such as our incredible GPS devices, must take these subtle effects into consideration to enable them to work effectively and precisely.

At slow speeds or with small variations in height, sophisticated instruments are needed to detect any differences in the flow of time, but the faster things go, the more dramatic the effects. For instance, many of us may remember hearing, somewhere or another, perhaps in science class in high school or college, that if someone could travel to the nearest star and back at anywhere near the speed of light, when they returned to earth all of their immediate family and friends would have passed away and they would arrive sometime in our planet's future. It is because near the speed of light, time comes almost to a complete stand still, and at the speed of light it actually comes to a complete stop. Along that line of thought, if you were hypothetically traveling on a beam of light (particles in the photon field) there would be no time at all, as strange and confusing as it is to imagine, time doesn't exist at the speed of light or in the photon field.

As you may know, black holes are a region of space where the gravitational field is so intense that the particles making up matter (usually coming in as stars) can't be prevented from a total collapse. Everything is annihilated back into pure primal space. A black hole is a little like revisiting the beginning of the Universe when everything was unified and infinitely compact in what is called, in the case of a black hole, a singularity.

From the outside looking in, anything falling into a black hole (a hypothetical clock perhaps) seems to continually slow down and eventually seems to stop just before it enters. This is due to the intense gravity in the surrounding area that slows the outgoing information to a virtual standstill. But, if it were possible for any of us to be unlucky enough to be travelling in a spacecraft getting pulled into a black hole, we would not notice any difference in the flow of time. Or if we managed to escape somehow just before we were about to enter into the black hole, we would come out of its gravitational field into the surrounding space's future. Again, this is because the flow of time is affected by the amount of mass and energy in the space in which it is manifesting, and a black hole is loaded with both.

As previously mentioned, time is an aspect of space, and not separate from it any more than the flow of a river is a separate aspect of the river in which that flow is being created. And to push the metaphor, consider the fact that within the flow of a river there are places where the water flows faster or slower depending on the surrounding conditions, just as time does. That being said, time is an extraordinary aspect of space, and obviously is a very hard thing to even vaguely understand. (But one thing we do know—time is money. Sorry bad joke!)

Getting back to the regular old space we are accustomed to, the space between you and what you are reading, that seemingly empty space, oddly, must contain all the information that enables us to experience right now all that is happening around us. Every speck of space is like a hologram containing all the information regarding how to make a Universe: the fundamental forces and their strengths, along with the qualities of particles, such as their size, spin, and the value of their charges, along with their quantity, ratio to each other, and how they will decay into other particles (for starters). All that predetermined information is contained in the space that is around and inside of you; it has to be, because if it wasn't there, and if that vast amount of information was localized in just some section of the original space of the Universe, the Universe wouldn't be as uniform as it is. It would be just a big incoherent mess. The Universe would be wildly different everywhere within it, with all the ratios of particles and the strength of the forces different and unevenly distributed without any sort of harmonious relationships between them.

Space's initial expansion, interestingly, occurred faster than the speed of light. So oddly, only space itself can travel faster than the speed of light, but nothing inside of it can. And after the exceedingly brief period of inflation, space's expansion slowed down at a predetermined time (no one at this time really knows exactly why the Universe's expansion slowed and just didn't keep going on and on, like we might logically assume it should have).

To top off all this cosmological predetermination that went on, each of these particles that ended up springing into existence, had for some unknown reason, an antiparticle created with an opposite charge at the same time. This strange creation of particle pairs, and not just one particle at a time, is a fundamental law of physics. It always happens, and has been continually experimentally verified. So after these particles had instantaneously coalesced out of space into quarks and then into protons and neutrons along with their corresponding anti-protons and anti-neutrons, they obliterated each other as they collided. These collisions, by the way, created the photons that we can still see with our sophisticated instruments in the background radiation coming at us from all directions in space. Unexpectedly, back in the good old days, our childhood TVs could pick up a very small percentage of this radiation when the channels were blank.

What is truly astonishing is that "one in a billion" of these particles were spared annihilation. We now call those particles matter. If this highly unlikely particle-antiparticle discrepancy had not have happened, our Universe would have been nothing but an extraordinarily large volume of space full of photons (light). And once again, we have no idea why or how this came to be, because this oddity defies the basic tenets of known physics. Perhaps cosmologists will come to understand why this happened at some time in the future, but this will not make it any less improbable and remarkable.

Another in our list of incredible things that needed to have happened for us to be here, is that if most of these newly created fundamental constants or forces of nature embedded in space were off by just a hair in their values, the whole house of cards would have fallen apart, and the Universe would be null and void, just a big waste of time and space.

It is in places like these that evidence of an underlying spiritual dynamic has emerged and the multi-verse advocates are compelled to make their point – their point being that there must be an infinite number of Universes that have been created to have achieved these wildly improbable effects, and we live, obviously, in one fit for life (mystery solved!). But again, why are there Universes period, and why do any of these remarkable things we call Universes have any of the qualities in place that we have been talking about?

We can think of it this way, as the physicist Paul Davis has done: it's a little like when the Universe was created, a metaphorical slot machine containing at least twenty-five gears with the spinning faces representing the multiple-potential values of the particles and forces that we now find in the Universe, was suddenly put into play. The lever was pulled at the point of creation and when the gears stopped spinning they all lined up and came out exactly right (Jackpot! We get to exist). Ask yourselves honestly, what are the odds of that happening, all those fundamental constants and their fine-tuned values coming into existence and turning out just right? Would you even put a nickel into a slot machine where the chances of winning were so incredibly low? Why bother? Of course, cosmically speaking the metaphorical universal slot machine with all those spinning dials would had to have sprung into existence out of nothing, somehow ready to be played.

Another odd aspect to all of this is that a lot of necessary properties, for us to be here, were hidden to begin with, and only emerged or came into existence after a period of time had elapsed and certain conditions were met. There is a long list of such things that we will encounter in the upcoming essays. The point I'm belaboring is, nothing should be taken for granted-as something that needed to have happened. There really should be absolutely nothing; there is really no obvious reason for a Universe to exist.

So after this quick cursory look at space and time, let's move on and take a closer look in the next essay at the bizarre array of particles that the Universe has produced.

THREE

THE PARTICLES

One of the many remarkable aspects of the Universe is that the amount of mass it contains is exactly the same amount as its gravitational energy. What this means is that the total amount of energy in the Universe comes out to be zero when everything in the Universe is taken into consideration – added up so to speak; mass being considered a positive, due to having "borrowed" its existence from the energy of space, and gravitation being the negative effect on the space in which it emerged. The Universe has been glibly said to be the ultimate free lunch, by physicist Alan Guth (the conceptual father of the inflationary hypothesis). That being so, there was still, we are told, a certain amount of energy required to get the whole thing started. The energy, it has been calculated, that produced the inflationary expansion was about the same amount as you might find in a couple of candy bars. We don't know where that trace amount of extra energy came from (the same place as the Universe in general—we can safely assume), and it is one of the many odd, if small, mysteries that have remained unsolved.

Mass and energy, both essentially being the same thing, generate gravity (and slow time, remember?) and if you think of particles as being minute energized points in the abundance of the different fields pervading space, as we have talked about, that makes sense. We can imagine that when the particles coalesced out of the energy that was essentially an aspect of space to begin with, it could be thought of as putting something like a torque on the space from which the energy is drawn up into those particles. That torque, a minute warping on the surrounding space is what we call gravity. (At least that's one way to look at it.) So when we read that almost infinite heat and energy filled all space in the beginning, the point that space is that energy, and that energy isn't something that is separate and contained in space, isn't usually fully realized. Also the fact is that this energized-expanding space was full of virtual particles (still is) and these inherent particles, which are embedded in the fabric of space, used and needed that initial burst of extravagant energy contained in space to maintain their existence.

By the way, the space surrounding you right now still has particles that are coming in and out of existence briefly and fleetingly. The reason they don't become permanently manifested is a lack of energy to sustain them, so they remain hidden. If a tremendous amount of energy was applied to a small portion of space in front of you, the ephemeral particles in that space would go from virtual to actual and continue to exist.

Interestingly, the familiar particles (protons and neutrons, that were once thought to be solid and fundamental) were fairly recently discovered to be themselves made up of much smaller particles that are whimsically called quarks (pertaining to a verse in the book Finnegan's Wake). And, of course, it goes without saying that these newly discovered quarks had to have been created with all the right qualities to enable them to manifest as larger particles, and to be in the right ratios so there wouldn't be any unused and left over lonely quarks roaming free. That little fireball of a Universe had a lot of richly detailed subtlety in it waiting to be expressed.

Let's ponder quarks for a minute. Quarks are a peculiar phenomenon. To start with, they are unimaginably small, and there are six different types, with different charges, that are in fractions no less, like-1/3 or +2/3 for instance. They bunched up into threes after the Universe had cooled enough to allow them to from its early intensely hot plasma-like state. (Why did all this happen? Like everything else, it's a compelling mystery!)

The three quarks that make up a proton, for instance, have a net positive charge when their charges are added up, and get this: quarks would be the size of specks of dust, if the protons they comprise were hypothetically enlarged to the size of our entire solar system. Think about that for a moment. The basic particles of matter are in essence almost nothing, mere swirling specks. The reason they appear to be something is that they are whirling in a defused, cloud-like manner at billions of times a second within the protons and neutrons.

That cloud-like effect is what makes the protons and neutrons appear to be solid; they are anything but solid. It would seem that the energy taken from the space the particles occupy is in large measure used as kinetic energy (the energy of motion).

To manifest as protons and neutrons the quarks are held in place in their turbulent swirling activity by the strong nuclear force that had (luckily) also just come into existence at the same time they had. The strong force is a manifestation of the exchange of force-carrying particles called gluons between the quarks. This is another odd and hard to comprehend feature of the quantum world: that subatomic forces are generated by the exchange of particles that contain that force-technically called gauge bosons.

The lines of force generated by the exchange of gluons between the quarks are astonishingly powerful. And the force gluons produce has the unlikely and remarkable quality of becoming more powerful when the quarks they hold together are being separated (just the opposite of all the other forces that diminish with distance). The binding force they create is so powerful in fact, that if you put two jumbo jets on a runway (hypothetically of course) and sent them off in opposite directions, they wouldn't even come close to being able to pull apart the quarks in a proton; they are basically inseparable.

This force, by the way, carries for only a very short distance and it "luckily" extends a little past the edge of the protons and neutrons, just far enough to keep the protons bound together in the nucleuses of the later-to-be-created atoms and elements. (Good foresight on the part of the quarks and gluons wouldn't you say?) That's because without the strong force's presence the positively charged protons would violently repel each other. This is another of the many aspects of the emerging Universe that had to be precisely exact, or nothing good, or for that matter bad, would happen.

Again, all these forces and particles and their interactions are coming together in just the right way (recurring theme) for us to later be thinking about it with these remarkably complex and highly improbable things we possess called brains, a brain that emerged down the line (13,8 billion years or so later) that generates the magic we are now experiencing as consciousness. What are the odds of that happening? Quarks to consciousness!

So let's briefly take stock for a moment at where we now find ourselves. We, at this time, have this long bewildering list of particles that had spontaneously emerged out of the fabric of space, or have now been created in collisions in nuclear particle accelerators. All these particles have different masses, or sometimes no mass at all like photons. They also have spins of different values or no spin, along with different charges or no charge. What is going on? This bewildering, confusing situation demanded some theoretical coherence, so physicists went to work to try to put it all together systematically, to create and put some sort of order into all of these disparate particles that were continually being discovered. After a lot of sharpening of their pencils (an old expression) and hard thinking, they were successful and came up with what is now called the standard model. After it was conceptualized and put together and the particles were put into ordered classes, the standard model was, over time, repeatedly experimentally verified. (It's remarkable how the Universe had done all this conceptualizing without the aide of any sharp pencils!)

This successful endeavor has been rightly considered one of humanities highest scientific achievements. It basically put all the particles into families and groups (hadrons, fermions and the like) making sense out of the mystifying array of the seemingly unrelated particles that were constantly being discovered in particle accelerators. Intriguingly, it would be found that unknown particles would sometimes be necessary to fill in a blank slot in the emerging model (something like how the periodic table was filled in with later-to-be-discovered elements). This was because of equations that had been created that would indicate a certain, as yet undiscovered, particle needed to be in existence to complete the emerging picture. They would inevitably find the missing particle after performing the appropriate experiment. A number of particles were discovered in this way (as was, in fact, the extraordinary existence of antimatter) and now, finally, all the slots have been filled.

Let's add another profound mystery to our ever-growing list: the fact that math equations reflect reality in such a compelling way. In the history of science, things have repeatedly been discovered on a mathematical level before they were later confirmed experimentally (the equations being sort of a map, before the scientists go on a quest of discovery). So in the Universe, which came first, the math or the matter? My guess is that Spirit clearly worked out the math first.

Anyway, soon the plot once again thickened, when it was realized that particles should not have any mass at all, and with that being the case, there was obviously a major component of the big picture that wasn't in place yet. So a new as yet undiscovered particle (field) was needed to give the other particles their mass (I'm not making this stuff up!). This is what came to be known as the Higgs boson (named after one of the guys who first realized it was a necessity). The Higgs boson, which was required to complete the picture, can be considered a particle/field that basically interacts with and puts a "drag" on the other particles, and that is what generates the other particle's mass. This effect is a little like the slowing effect when you throw a penny into a pool and the water slows it down on its way to the bottom.

Of course, physicists felt compelled to find the Higgs boson, so in Cern Switzerland, a big international consortium spent billions of dollars making a cyclotron powerful enough to hopefully find it (they were that sure of the math). And by gosh, once completed they cranked the thing up, and after a few stops and starts they did discover it, just in the energy range they thought it would be. This was a very big deal (The God Particle, it was ludicrously called); front-page news.

This apparatus by the way, the cyclotron, is huge and is one of the most complicated devices ever devised and created by humans, and it certainly cost a lot. It is basically a circular track or tube (almost 17 miles) where they speed up particles, electromagnetically, and smash them together near the speed of light and evaluate the damage done (the particle debris generated) with high-tech recording sensors. Pull up a picture online and look at the wiring – amazing electrical engineering (and I used to have a hard time connecting up my stereo speakers).

The discovery of the Higgs boson capped off the standard model (at least for now) and a lot of what makes up the Universe was starting to be understood, but then something strange happened—it always does! Cosmologists began to realize that what we see out there and around us makes up shockingly only about 4 percent of the Universe. The rest has been, unimaginatively, called dark energy and dark matter. When the results were in and finalized, dark matter was discovered to make up around 25 percent of the mass-energy density of the Universe and dark energy (generating the accelerating expansion of space, therefore the Universe) the other 70 percent or so. All this just turned up unexpectedly, and just when we thought that we (not me, of course) were starting to get it figured out! We should have known better. We will talk about dark energy and matter in later essays, but first let's look at the fundamental forces that came together in just the right way to make it all happen.

FOUR

THE FORCES

In the initial little speck of almost infinitely hot Universe, there were some things immediately present that would determine its fate, without which, the space-time that had just emerged would become an expansive lifeless void. A few of these necessary things (as far as allowing us to be here now) are what we now consider the Laws of Nature. Let's take a look at them.

There are four fundamental forces that have advantageously organized the Universe for life. Why there are only four and not more or less we have no idea, but we do know they work and we do know they were part of the information package included in our resourceful Universe. We can only be grateful that they exist and are manifested with their particular strengths and ranges of effect. They are: gravity, the strong and weak nuclear forces and electromagnetism (at one time this now single force was considered to be two separate ones).

As in virtually everything that is a basic constituent of the Cosmos, if the intensity of any of these forces were adjusted just slightly up or down, you would get a Universe that is radically different from the one in which we find ourselves. And let's be honest, there is absolutely no reason, at all, for them to exist, let alone have their life-supporting-finely-tuned values. Let's very briefly consider them individually.

We'll start with gravity, the weakest force by far and the first force to be given a numerical value; as you may know, this was done by Isaac Newton. But even though he could see and measure the effects of gravity, he was totally bewildered by what he called this "action from a distance." The problem being: how could an object (a planet for instance), affect another object (the moon) through empty space. It didn't make any sense as to how that could possibly happen. For a few hundred years the fundamental nature of this force remained a complete mystery.

It wasn't until Einstein's Theory of Relativity that an explanation was offered that gave a coherent, but bizarre clarification as to how gravity creates its effects. Einstein's remarkable insight was that matter curves space, and gravity basically is the effect of warped space. Of course, this didn't make any sense either at the time it was originally proposed, and had to be experimentally verified (by the observation of starlight curving around the sun during a solar eclipse) before it started to became widely accepted in the scientific community, because common sense told everyone, after all, that space was nothing.

So, first of all, as previously mentioned, the strength of gravity could have been any value. And now we know that if it were a little less, the stars and planets would not have formed. The same disruptive type of thing would happen, but in the opposite direction if Nature had amped up the strength of gravity a bit. The Universe after springing into existence would have immediately, or shortly thereafter, imploded back into itself, and that would have certainly put an early unhappy end to it all. Also, if it was just a little more intense, stars would have evolved too quickly and there wouldn't have been enough time for life to have developed on any of a star's surrounding planets. For us to be here, gravity really has to be just right (like you know whose porridge). And clearly it is.

Moving along: the next force to emerge out of the rapidly cooling, but still red hot Universe immediately after the Big Bang was what is now called the strong force. As mentioned in a previous essay, the strong force is unbelievably powerful, to the point that it essentially can't be broken. You'll remember that it holds those fast moving quarks together through the exchange of gluons. Fortunately, some of this force leaks out of the protons and neutrons and this little leakage enables atomic nucleuses to stay together and not get blown apart, as they would and should if just subject to the repulsion effect of the same positive electrical charges of the other protons.

As a quick aside, charge is a property of matter that on its most fundamental level cannot really be explained and it must just be taken as a given aspect of certain particles (quarks to began with) in Nature. No one knows why quarks have charge, but without this intrinsic and mysterious characteristic, atoms could not possibly exist along with just about everything else. Another thing worthy of note about the charge values of the different particles is that if you add them all up (the positive and the negative charges found in Nature), it comes out to zero charge in the same way gravity and mass cancel each other out. So again, when taken as a whole the entire Universe adds up to zero. Double zeros in fact! A Universe adding up to nothing coming from nothing! What is the likelihood of that happening? Perhaps you might think it is basically zero – but against the odds it conspicuously did happen.

Back to the strong force; if the strong force was a little more intense, all the hydrogen now being used as fuel in the stars, our sun included, would have immediately bonded together and the Universe would be filled with stars made of Helium, but with no hydrogen available to make water.

So what would happen, you might ask, if the strong force didn't exist all of a sudden? Well, everything (atoms, protons, neutrons and the quarks comprising them) would blow apart! The Universe simply doesn't work without these extraordinary things we call the Laws of Nature

Now on briefly to the weak force; the weak force only resides within atoms and doesn't extend beyond them. It is responsible for the fission process (the breaking apart of atomic nuclei) that takes place in radioactive decay in general and spectacularly in supernovas in particular. This force allows atoms to change into different more electrically stable isotopes (elements with different charges due to different amounts of electrons, protons and neutrons in them). In a way, within atoms it competes with the strong force and wins out occasionally. The weak force wins when atoms with bulky nucleuses, those with very large numbers of protons and neutrons, break up (like uranium for instance). This splitting apart of nuclei is triggered by the exchange of a boson (a force carrying packet of energy) moving from a proton to a neutron or vice versa. This whole process is to create more electrically stable nuclei. The problem with radioactivity, as far as we humans are concerned, is that the ejected part of the nucleus can whack our DNA and create cancerous mutations.

By the way, when neutrons and protons were created initially out of quarks, the neutrons started immediately decaying into protons and would have decayed out of existence within about 10 minutes if they had not coupled up with protons. So there are no neutrons all by themselves roaming in empty space. (I'll bet you never thought about that!)

The weak force, as all the others, if dialed up or down just a very small percent would change everything. For instance, if it were a little more powerful, stars would burn too quickly, and neutrinos would be trapped inside the cores of stars during supernova explosions, and this subtlety would not permit the stars to completely blow apart. Exploding stars also don't take place if the force is too weak, but for a completely different reason. Who cares, right? Well-you should, at least a little.

Supernovas are important because without them and (come to find out) colliding neutron stars, all the heavier elements would just stay locked up in dead stars and that would be another potential ending point in the march toward complexity. That is because, a whole host of the heaviest elements (everything heavier that iron) that make up a large part of what we experience, are produced in the first split second within these colossal-supernova blasts that blow apart stars. These heavier more complex elements, along with all the rest, are then spread out in space and reassembled in the next generation of stars and their planets, such as our very own Sun and Earth (these unlikely but fundamentally important supernova events will be discussed in more depth in up coming essays).

The next and the last force to emerge was electromagnetism. And let there be light! It is a good thing Nature didn't forget to imbed this force field with its inherent particles into the fabric of space. Without it, nothing interesting or even remotely worthwhile would have taken place (as far as we're concerned). There would be no sun, star or moonlight; no computers, TVs or radios; no this, that and the other thing we enjoy so much. You get the point; the electromagnetic field and its force-carrying particles are special to us, and the Universe would be a dud without them.

Not too long ago, physicists managed to combine electromagnetism with the weak force, and so, in a way, we are down to just three basic forces of nature, at least at very high temperatures. One of the goals of theoretical physicists is to combine all the forces into just one. This will no doubt happen sometime in the not-so-distant future (and may that Force be with you!).

Something About Light

It is worthy of repeating that if you were to hypothetically take a ride on a photon, time would not exist. You could go (on your photon) from one end of the Universe to the other in no time at all. That would mean that on some level the Universe doesn't really exist, at least spatially from a photon's perspective. (You could say that the reason nothing can travel faster than the speed of light is that at the speed of light no movement, time or speed exists-they only appear to from our limited perspective.) It is almost as if the interface between the Universe, and the Infinite that is manifesting it, is to be found here in some hard to determine way.

It is interesting to note that mystics throughout the ages have quite often claimed to have had experienced the hidden spiritual force within Nature as an uplifting encounter with light. That, perhaps, makes a little more sense from what we have just discussed.

There, somewhat entertainingly, has now emerged the possibility of a fifth force in Nature. This force seems to be responsible for the recently discovered accelerating expansion of space, a sort of anti-gravity repulsive force whose effects until recently had remained another hidden aspect of the seemingly dull emptiness of space. It is called the dark force. Let's explore the dark force in our next essay.

FIVE

DARK ENERGY

When some of us were first starting to read books on astronomy as teenagers, the common consensus was that sometime in the distant future the Universe would stop its expansion and collapse back into itself, through the slowing and contracting effect of gravity. This inevitable collapse was called The Big Crunch, a final culmination to the Big Bang. There was all sorts of speculation about the results of this contraction, one of them being on the flow of time (that it would be reversed). Some speculated that after the crunching was complete another Universe would exit on the other side, so to speak, and another Big Bang would start the whole thing over again as part of an infinite series of similar events.

The Universe from that perspective was eternal, with no need of a Creator, so many liked to think. That was a fairly simple idea compared to the one now employed to refute the need of a Creator—the "multiverse" (an "infinite" amount of

Universes having been created to account for all the fine-tuned subtleties now being uncovered in our fortunate one). This, by the way, is a direct refutation of a guiding light in scientific investigations-Occam's razor, which is basically the search for the simplest explanation for any known phenomenon, not the most complex one that can possibly be imagined.

So consider the surprise when it was discovered a few years ago that instead of slowing down, the expansion rate of the Universe was actually accelerating. This finding baffled the scientific community; it came as a complete shock. On the bright side, it was another inexplicable unsolved mystery to employ and occupy scientists and graduate students for years to come.

Well, it turns out that this so-called dark energy behind the expansion makes up a whopping 70 percent of the Universe's inherent energy. It also has to be adjusted to a level that makes all the other aspects of the Universe's fine-tuning pale into insignificance. The amount of energy in space for the expansion rate to work as it does comes in at a mind-boggling 10 to the 120th power "less" than what was calculated and expected to be found in space (this expected figure was derived in part from the values of the virtual particles inherent in space); that is a 1 with 120 zeros after it.

So, here we go again, when everything is taken into consideration, without this "exact" number the Universe doesn't work at all as far as being fit for life. The space within it would have expanded too fast, and if this energy intrinsic in space was off even a little, 1 to the 120th for instance, the Universe would end up being just ever rapidly-expanding-featureless-empty space. This fact is literally inconceivably improbable and is a deep unexplained mystery at this point. From that perspective, it has been said, without any exaggeration, that the Universe as we know it is balanced on a razor's edge of improbability (try writing a 120 zeros on a piece of paper and think about it for a moment).

With those kind of odds, you would assume that anyone aware of them would have to at least admit, or perhaps consider, that the numbers are starting to suggest that there is something extraordinary going on here. But as in all things, people get locked into their mindsets, and even with overpowering evidence they rationalize their previously held positions. Reason knows its destination before it begins its journey, it has been said. By the way, the number mentioned above is the statistical-probability equivalence of doing a coin toss and it coming up heads or tails 400 times in a row (Physicist Paul Davis did the math, not me). That is basically the improbability of our existence and just pertains to that particular fact alone.

All this is strange to be sure, but to my mind one of the strangest aspects of this expansion of space is that as space enlarges, the space that has been recently created (somehow and everywhere) has all the same properties and energy levels as the preexisting space. Perhaps the extra energy derived from the newly created space is what is driving the increasing expansion rate.

So, at this time, there are only speculative hypotheses about what this energy is and what seems to cancel the calculated inherent energy of space down to a level that allows the Universe to exist as we are now experiencing it.

What we do know is that the Universe is not going to collapse back into itself, and that this Universe only happened once. (There may be others, why not? But we will never know for sure.) We also know its expansion rate is speeding up, and every 10 billion years or so it will have doubled in size.

And to think, we once thought of space as being a big blank nothing. Space is something that is really quite extraordinary. And adding to all the other extraordinary hidden aspects of space is that it contains another mystery called dark matter. Let's take a look at that next. Actually we can't take a look; it can't be seen!

SIX

DARK MATTER

It wasn't too long ago that it was noticed through the analysis of the rotational speed of the stars in distant galaxies that the ones on the outer edges were moving way too fast for them to stay gravitationally bound to those galaxies; the stars through the centrifugal force of their movements should have been jettisoned out into the surrounding space. Galaxies, it was realized, should and really could not exist if the only effect on them was the gravitational force generated by the observable mass within them.

This was hard to accept to say the least, but after this unanticipated fact was repeatedly verified, the cosmologists were compelled to try to figure out what the missing mass was that was producing this observable effect. Of course, they initially thought it would be something they already knew existed, like dead or dimly lit stars or maybe just dust, gas and cosmic debris in general. They found a little of what they were looking for, but not nearly enough of any of it to even put a dent in the amount of matter necessary to pull off what was required to generate the effects they had been observing. The necessary amount was estimated to be at least 5 or 6 times that which could be observed and accounted for.

So after all other known possibilities had been exhausted, the only alternative left was that it was something that could not be directly detected; something that didn't interact with normal matter except gravitationally, much in the same way that neutrinos don't interact with normal matter, for instance.

So, after the cosmologists explored a lot of competing hypotheses (theories in progress), the common consensus now is that the missing mass is "probably" generated by an invisible particle that was created near the initial point of creation with all the others. Most physicists believe it to be a particle that didn't decay (lose mass) for some as yet unknown reason, and it is a manifestation of yet another field that is intrinsic to space-time. They call these hypothetical entities WIMPS (weakly-interacting-massive particles).

Regardless, if they ever find more than circumstantial evidence of these particles (and they are working hard at it), what should get our attention, as much as anything, is once again the Universe was created with something that after some time would make its effect felt, and that without that something having just the right amount of consequence, in this case gravitational strength, the Universe we know would unravel.

What seems to be a possibility is that the particles that are speculated to make up dark matter are somehow affected only by the weak force, enabling them to form a loose fog-like body resembling the halo around a light on a foggy night. It is within these halos or pockets of dark matter that stars and galaxies reside.

The WIMPS are speculated to have enough mass and interact just enough with each other to facilitate these unseen and undetectable particles coming together, but not enough to get them to coalesce into much smaller star-like structures as normal matter does, because of the fact that normal matter is subject to the strong force that binds protons and neutrons together.

Well, it will be awhile before cosmologists figure out exactly what dark matter is. What we do know is that without it there would be no stars or galaxies or us, and there is a lot more of it than normal-everyday matter. This is a perplexing mystery remaining to be solved. The Universe continues to offer up unforeseen surprises.

Fortunately, one thing we know quite a bit about are the atoms that make up the world around us which, unexpectedly wind up being just around 2 percent of what we now believe comprises the observable Universe. These everyday atoms are truly remarkable and exhibit all sorts of emergent and surprising qualities. We will look at some of those interesting characteristics in our next essay.

SEVEN

ATOMS

It was all so simple when we were young. Atoms were like a tiny solar system. They had a nucleus made of something and small balls of something else whirling around them, we all saw the pictures. We assumed they had always existed, having never thought about it. It was the atomic age when some of us were kids. Back then the hidden energies within the atom had just been released, and that was both a good thing and a very bad thing for all the obvious reasons: progress versus annihilation.

Once again, just when it was thought to have been figured out, things were not as simple as they seemed. We know now that atoms didn't always exist. There was a time in the history of the Universe when there were no atoms at all. We also now know that the simplistic atoms, as we used to see them represented, are much more complicated than we could ever have imagined.

As we have seen in the previous essays, there was the confinement of particles called quarks into protons and neutrons. Some protons remained isolated, while others coupled up quickly with the rapidly decaying neutrons (to make deuterium) thanks to the seepage of the powerfully adhesive strong force. Then a spilt second later most of the deuterium joined up with other deuterium particles to make what would wind up being the nucleuses of helium (which now makes up about 25 percent of the atomic mass in the Universe).

The Helium nuclei with their two protons and two neutrons were as far as the nucleuses of the emerging elements could go for the time being. This was because of the early expanding Universe's diminishing heat and pressure that was necessary to get them to bond together. The entire Universe at that point was like the interior of the sun. The rest of the elements and their more complex nucleuses, like carbon, oxygen and all the others, wouldn't come into existence until much later on through the evolution of stars and the supernova explosions that took place within some of those stars.

As the Universe continued to cool and expand over time (about 380,000 years or so), it was at a temperature that allowed the freely circulating electrons that had also inexplicably emerged out of space along with the other basic particles, to finally attach themselves to the existing nuclei and make some of the simpler atoms.

If we think about it, we might assume that the electrons would have immediately just plowed into the protons, and that would have been the end of them (from the powerful pull of their opposite attracting electrical charges). That's what common-sense-everyday physics tell us should have happened; but surprisingly it didn't. That is because when electrons come in to close proximity to protons and neutrons, they disperse out into cloud-like structures (this fortunate characteristic of electrons is due to a mysterious quantum effect). It takes extreme force, usually in the form of intense gravity inside stars, to get electrons into contact with protons nucleuses to create neutrons. So, when the universe had calmed and cooled a little, this absolutely essential quantum effect pertaining specifically to electrons came into play.

We need to stop for a moment and think about how and why these wildly improbable, mathematically sophisticated quantum effects came into existence at the exact time they were needed, so to speak. And to fully realize that without these effects in place, the universe, once again, falters in its "drive" toward complexity, and nothing even remotely interesting happens (again, is this fact just pure random chance?).

Anyway, after the electrons are in place around the nucleuses, along comes another quantum effect: the Pauli exclusion principle. This, simply put, means that fermions (electrons and quarks) take up space (some particles by the way don't take up space, like photons, because they have no mass), and are excluded from being in the exact same spot or position doing the same thing, at the same time, as another fermion.

This intrinsic aspect of electrons came in handy, preventing them from piling up in the lowest orbitals of atoms. Two electrons (and that is all there can be in the closest orbital) have to spin in different directions (one of their bizarre qualities), or they can't cohabit in what is called the same shell together. (I told you it was more complicated than we had thought.) How does one electron determine to spin in the opposite direction that allows it to team up in the same orbital space? They must sense and affect each other somehow and then Nature forces them into their different directional spins. (Spin, by the way, on a quantum level has more to do with a property exhibited by particles than an actual spinning motion, as we would usually think of it).

Physicists are like lawyers somewhat, in that they have developed their own words and language to confuse the rest of us.

These surprising things called orbitals, found within atoms that have also spontaneously emerged as an inherent quality of the Universe, come in different shapes, sizes and orientations in space. And the farther they spread out from the nucleus, the more electrons there can be in that larger volume of space (finally something that makes a little sense).

The orbitals can be roughly conceptualized as looking something like balloons of different sizes and shapes attached to the top of a stick (it should always be taken into consideration that metaphors always break down on a quantum level) bound together at their tied-off openings at the top point of the stick, (let's go all the way and put a little metaphorical ball at the end of this now invisible stick), where they are all attached as roughly representing the nucleus. The more electrons there are in the atom, the more blurry-balloon-like shapes there are at different distances, shapes and angles from the nucleus.

Electrons always fill these orbitals from the bottom up, so to speak, because they must if that level isn't full. In the process of dropping down into the lower adjacent shell they give off a photon (those little wave-like packets of energy). The photons coming out of the atoms in this process have different wavelengths and magnitudes and hence give off different colors depending on what orbital they drop down from. (And the Lord said "Let there be light, and let's make it timeless and colorful too!")

All this is intricate stuff to be sure that we are just touching upon, and should not in any way be taken for granted. There is nothing that had gone on beforehand to even remotely indicate that this would be the case of how electrons would arrange themselves around the nucleuses once space had cooled off a bit. It is an aspect of the Universe, as so many others, that can be compared analogously to an undeveloped negative going through the process of becoming gradually visible in a dark room; the information on the negative of what the picture is going to be is already there, but unmanifested and invisible, it just needs time to develop. All aspects of how the Universe emerges are hidden until they spontaneously spring into existence, and for the most part, should be considered unpredictable.

Most aspects of the developing Universe aren't evident as even remote possibilities, let alone probabilities, until they're expressed (they only appear to be part of some sort of inevitable logical progression when viewed retrospectively). This is a major point that should never be forgotten as we go along. When we study these types of things in school we become so preoccupied with learning all this difficult stuff that we lose track of how improbable and really miraculous (if you want to look at it that way) it all is.

So in this case, electrons fortunately stay out of the nucleus when they spread out like clouds after being pulled toward the nucleus by that mysterious quality we call charge, and they accumulate in orbitals in mathematically determined groupings, based on intricate principles and laws inherent in Nature. There is no reason any of that should surprise us – right?

One of the strangest things about atoms is that as they go through the process of filling their orbitals and accumulating more protons, neutrons and electrons when they are being forged in stars, they change into different elements. These different elements that fall into groupings, have completely different characteristics from each other. Bear in mind they are made of basically the same things, just more of the same things. Think of the difference between gold and lead for instance, or helium and uranium. Is there anything else in Nature that comes to mind, where when more of the same type of material is added, that material is transformed into something with radically different qualities, characteristics and attributes? It is truly remarkable that atoms transform like that just because they have added more protons, neutrons and electrons.

You might ask yourself, how were all those complex different elements, once they were created in stars dispersed into space? (I know, you probably didn't.) We will explore how anyway in an up coming essay. But first we will take a brief look back into the quantum level of atoms and another bizarre and remarkable phenomenon: quantum tunneling that has been, surprisingly, found to be needed to pull off the more interesting aspects of the Universe.

EIGHT

QUANTUM LEVEL MYSTERIES

The space and forces within the atom, the quantum level of the Universe, has slowly been revealing some of its non-intuitive aspects over the last hundred years or so. Much of that which has emerged was totally unanticipated and baffling. But from another perspective, it shouldn't be all that surprising; the Universe makes up, and plays by its own rules as it unfolds, and everything about it should, at least, seem a little strange to us.

Our brains, and therefore our thinking, are conditioned by evolution in the way they function on our everyday-mundane level, and we have strong binding intuitions about the way things ought to be. But it is always to be remembered that nothing necessarily should be the way it is; when we opened our eyes to the world around us at birth, we just immediately started accepting it as is. Why wouldn't we? So on a quantum level, when something doesn't make sense, and cannot be conceptualized with some metaphor from this realm in which we live, it shouldn't come as too big a surprise. The brilliant and entertaining physicist Richard Feynman once said, "I can safely say that nobody understands quantum mechanics." He was right!

If you think about it for a moment, it is really incredible that we understand anything at all about what goes on in that small of a scale. A number of the discoveries that have been made, once again, were deemed necessary because of the mathematical equations that had been done, before they were later experimentally verified. I have talked to people who make the claim that some phenomenon can only be understood mathematically; words alone cannot convey what they are trying to describe. Take a look some time at the math equations that define some area or aspect of physics and think for a moment about how odd it is that physical reality can be explained in that abstract-foreign-mathematical form of language. It really is quite extraordinary.

There is an old quote attributed to Einstein (He has the best quotes, doesn't he?): "The most incomprehensible thing about the Universe is that it is comprehensible." And we might add that without mathematics it isn't. There is an amusing story, supposedly true, about a tribe somewhere or other that only had three numbers, one, two and many. We have arrived into a place that is a long way from there.

In other essays, a number of peculiar things that happen in this subatomic domain have been mentioned, for instance, electrons jumping from one atomic orbital to the next instantaneously, without any intermediate transition occurring. (By the way, the photon given off in this transition is the quanta of energy from which quantum physics derives its name.) Another example is the way electrons disperse into cloud like formations in the quantum realm with no particle aspect to them until they are observed. We could also mention the oddity of the instantaneous transfer of information between two polarized-entangled photons faster than the speed of light. The list goes on, but the tunneling aspect of particles is particularly strange and at the same time absolutely necessary for our existence. Here's why: when particles are not being measured they travel through their respective fields as somewhat diffused waves (a little like when you can see something moving just below the surface of water and can't tell where it is exactly). These waves are elongated, so before they are observed or measured in some way, the particle-potential aspect of the wave resides in any number of places within that wave, it only consolidates or collapses into its particle aspect when it gets measured or is brought into existence in some other way. And (this is important) just because its position in a certain part of the wave is at a low probability, it does not mean that it will not be found there. So because the particle/wave is spread out, when it encounters any sort of barrier, there is a part of it that has the possibility of being found partially through any obstruction it encounters. It has tunneled through, so to speak, and even though there is a very low probability of the particle aspect of the wave being on the other side of the barrier, it is still remotely possible. The probability of this happening, by the way, is like winning the lottery three times in a row – very unlikely, but it can happen.

Even with the odds so steeply stacked against its occurrence, it does happen in inconceivable large numbers in the sun. The hydrogen atoms (protons), in their wave aspect, can extend or tunnel through the positively charged force-field barriers of the other protons; this enables them to come within range of each other's strong force and fuse and form helium nucleuses. Without this highly unlikely quantum phenomenon, nuclear fusion and the energy it produces would not take place within the sun because the temperature and pressure, though extreme, isn't sufficient to breach this barrier; the repulsive electrical force is too strong to allow it to happen. And it is only because of the inconceivably large numbers of protons within the stars that allows the incredibly steep odds of it happening to be overcome, and to have the star radiate out some of it's energy through the process of nuclear fusion. Thus, without this wildly counter-intuitive-quantum tunneling taking place, there would be no warming sunlight, just cold dark space in a cold dark Universe.

So we have to put quantum tunneling somewhere near the top of our ever-growing list of improbable emergent necessities in order for us to be here trying to understand it.

NINE

THE FIRST STARS

The Universe had turned unimaginably cold and dark once the initial energetic burst put forth at the point of creation had started to subside; it was basically smooth and black with only small disparities in its density here and there. These small differences were relics generated by the quantum fluctuations within that initial speck of space "at the beginning of time" when the Universe was smaller than an atom.

Without the inexplicable dark matter we assume exists, the Universe would have just continued to expand and cool and that would have been the end of the story. No stars, galaxies or galactic clusters would have formed, just defused hydrogen and helium, with a few other lightweight elements thrown into the mix. This mixture would have simply dispersed evenly out into space, with the space that contained it spreading out into the Infinite.

Dark energy, generating the accelerating expansion of space, wouldn't be much of a factor for billions of years. On the other hand, dark matter would start making its presence felt early on in that it had been slowly accumulating in the regions of space in which it had slightly higher concentrations. Gradually over hundreds of millions of years this process created large and small areas of it, which we now call halos.

We know dark matter, whatever it is exactly, does affect the space in which it is manifested. It generates a gravitational field, and these seedbeds facilitated the simple elements drifting freely in space to coalesce into incredibly large masses of hydrogen and helium gas, sometimes thousands of times larger than our very own star—the sun. These enormous masses of gas ended up being first generation short-lived stars (lasting just a few million years). If large enough, and perhaps most were, they became supernovas or even black holes

Black holes are what happens when the fusion process within enormous stars runs its course up through the elements, with the process stalling out with the non-fusible element iron. When iron makes up the bulk of the star's core, it can't generate any resistance in the form of radiant energy to counter the force being exerted by the gravitational pressure generated by the star's mass. At that point there is nothing to stop the star and the three-dimensionally curved space around it from imploding into itself and annihilating the fundamental particles and forces within the star. It collapses into something akin to the original space at the moment of creation – small, hot and loaded with unexpressed information.

We now know the Universe has billions of black holes dispersed throughout it. Most of them reside in the central areas of galaxies – our galaxy has one. Some, if not most, wind up containing the masses of thousands of stars. And when they are gorging themselves with stars that happen to be close enough to be drawn in, a tremendous amount of radiation is given off, broadcasting their presence. These outbursts of radiation are now considered to be the probable source of the mysterious, puzzling and fantastic levels of energy quasars are know to emit.

Stars that don't implode into black holes, if large enough, become supernovas. (Our sun by the way, will become a red giant and gradually enlarge and engulf the earth billions of years from now – all things must pass!)

Back to Supernovas: these events take place when the fusion process within the star runs its course up through the element of iron; just like in the formation of black holes. But in the case of supernovas the gravitational energy isn't as intense, though extreme, so a black hole doesn't happen. Surprisingly the star doesn't just gradually cool off and fade away, it instead catastrophically explodes. The remaining core of this explosion, by the way, becomes a neutron star, with the electrons having been crushed into the protons and the neutrons themselves compressed together. These remnant neutron stars are minuscule compared to the stars that generate them; they're generally about the size of big city, but they weigh more than our sun.

Time for some fun facts!

The sun, if you didn't know, could hold about 1,300,000 earths inside of it and weighs 333,000 times as much as the earth. Another thing of tangential interest is that with the sun being 93 million miles away from the earth, it takes sunlight over 8 minutes to get here. So for all we know, the sun went pitch-black 7½ minutes ago. A couple more facts I can't resist passing on: When you say "Hi, how are you doing?" to someone, a photon travelling at the speed of light (186,000 miles a second) could have gone around the earth about 14 times. And it takes light even at that implausible speed about 5½ hours to get to Pluto from here, and 4 years to get to the nearest star—Alpha Centauri. The Universe became a very big place over the years, wouldn't you say?

Back to stars. The star supporting fusion process gives off heat because when the nuclei of 2 hydrogen atoms, each usually containing 1 proton (and in the case of deuterium a neutron), fuse to make helium, the helium surprisingly ends up with less mass than the combined total of the 2 hydrogen nuclei that were forced together (1 + 1 = less than 2). This odd fact is fundamentally important to us being here. The superfluous mass left over for the fusion process is converted into energy and released in the form of photons (starlight) and neutrinos (those phantom ghost particles). These first-generation stars, as mentioned, didn't last long, but the Universe at least now had pockets of heat generating light and after some of the stars exploded, dust to work with (not bad for that initial speck of energized space).

Fortunately, most of the newly created stars weren't big enough to become black holes, but they were large enough to blow themselves apart and disperse their newly minted elements far and wide to generate the dust just mentioned. Neutrinos play a surprising and necessary part in the whole process of this dispersal of the elements, as we'll see in a later essay. But before we take a closer look at supernovas, let's look in more detail at the progression of the formation of the elements inside stars. There is a curious, and once hidden, bewildering aspect to it – actually, it's curious and bewildering, in the same way, as everything else we have been delving into.

TEN

THE BERYLLIUM BOTTLENECK?

You have probably never heard of it, but without it being "breached" in the progression of the creation of elements within stars, most of the elements beyond helium could not have been created, and once again the Universe would have stalled out at a level of low complexity, because after beryllium the next element forged by nuclear fusion within stars is carbon. And the workhorse carbon atom is the cornerstone of life forms as we know them.

The story is rather complicated and goes something like this: helium nuclei are extremely stable as far as nuclei go. So stable in fact, that for a while they were considered to be particles (alpha by name) in early experiments done by physicists. So when two helium nuclei smash together in the incredible heat and pressure that gravity produces in stars, it was assumed that the collision would also lead to another fairly stable nuclei. But in time it was realized that the beryllium nuclei that were created were anything but stable; it was revealed that they broke apart in 10 to the minus 17 seconds. So the puzzle was: how did the wildly unstable beryllium nuclei have enough time to add yet another helium nuclei to itself to make carbon? It was calculated to be statistically impossible for three helium nuclei to come together at the same exact moment and produce the amount of carbon known to exist in the Universe (quantum tunneling or not).

Fred Hoyle (who coined the once derisive term Big Bang – he hated the idea) was the physicist who realized that the carbon nucleus had to have a resonance (an excited state) that enables the seemingly impossible to happen.

A resonance is basically the vibrational rate of the nucleus; the rate of vibration varies in different types of nucleuses. A molecule's resonance has to add up to the combined rate of the two nucleuses coming together (in this case three) along with the kinetic energy of the collision that has taken place. You can imagine the math doesn't always add up, and this prevents some nucleuses from easily fusing. To add to the complexity, the nucleuses have within themselves the capacity to vibrate at different rates or levels, and can drop down to a lower level of vibration when conditions permit. This is somewhat similar to what an electron does when it drops down from the outer area of an atom to a lower shell or orbital and while in the process, emits energy in the form of a photon to change its energy level.

So Sir Fred (later knighted for this discovery and, later still, a begrudging accepter of the Big Bang Theory) assumed there must be an excited state of the carbon nucleus that had not at that time been discovered to enable its improbable, yet frequent, creation. He prodded the reluctant experimenters at Stanford where he was working at the time to look for it, and it was, to their surprise (not his) found to exist. He had done the math (there it is again) before the experiment because he had realized that without that specific level of resonance, carbon doesn't happen, or occurs only in minute-trace levels (the margin of error for the process to take place "without" the excited resonance state was only 4 percent). So because of the carbon nucleus's (lucky?) ability to exist at this higher state of excitation, it was much easier for carbon to be created by the combination of the kinetic energy of the collision, along with the inherent vibrational rates of the beryllium and helium nuclei.

But the plot once again thickens: oxygen's nucleuses resonate at around 1 percent lower than the combined nucleuses of the carbon and helium nuclei needed for its creation when coupled with the kinetic energy of the collisions necessary to create them (Who would have thought? It's almost like the Universe wanted to mess with the physicists it later was going to bring into existence). Because of this fact, the creation of oxygen is harder to come by, so this enables carbon to remain relatively abundant (almost all the carbon would have been converted to oxygen with little, if any, carbon left over, if oxygen's resonance had been just a little different). This is again fairly complicated stuff, and you can probably see by now that the odds are fairly steep for any of this taking place; we are after all dealing with just a few percentage points in the vibration rates in an assortment of different but common nucleuses, changing everything to come later. But the Universe wasn't worried; it was making up the rules as it went along (actually it had made them up in the beginning, before they were needed), or so it would seem by all the improbable, against-the-odds events needed to take place for us to be here, and to be somewhat confused thinking about it. The elements kept being forged through the fusion process up to iron; this was the end of the road for stars; no more fusion was possible in the prevailing conditions.

As I have previously mentioned in another essay, without something extraordinary taking place, the newly minted elements would have just stayed within the stars, and the stars would just burn out and become black heaps of nuclear ash. The Universe would have been just a bunch of dark-dead stars loaded with elements littering space, but the Universe had a very clever way of preventing this bleak scenario from happening. It would spread these elements out into space by exploding these stars in a surprisingly unlikely way, in an event that we now call a supernova. How and why did the stars explode? Let's take a look in the next essay.

ELEVEN

SUPERNOVAS

The Universe does a lot of strange things. One of its best tricks is how it gets stars to explode and spew out their contents for our later enjoyment, as well as for the enjoyment of all the other life forms that probably populate the Universe. The Universe doesn't have to do this, or anything else for that matter, but it does. Here we are, the byproduct of exploding stars. The brief how and why of exploding stars goes something like this: when nuclei are fused together in stars, as you will remember there is a little energy that is left over from the process and emitted, generating heat and light. There are remnants of the elements that have not been fused; these are some of the elements that are now making up your body.

Iron's creation, is as far up as the elements produced by the fusion process can go, and it ends there. In other words, iron nucleuses can't be fused together in a star (it simply takes too much energy to do it), and at that point there is nothing to keep the star from imploding into itself. The stage is now set for the cosmic fireworks to begin.

What happens next is that the surrounding gas rushes into the non-radiated space left when the fusion processes have stopped. The gas is coming in at a speed and force that is beyond imagination due to the vast gravitational force being applied to it. This violent blow presses the electrons down into the nucleuses in the iron core of the star, converting the protons into neutrons. The force of the incoming gas is so powerful, it crushes and compresses the nucleuses of the atoms of the star's core momentarily. But the core rebounds in spectacular fashion, sending a powerful and swift shock wave of energy through the collapsing star's gaseous envelope.

This series of events has almost enough energy to completely blow the star apart but not quite, because the shock wave would start to peter out after plowing through potentially hundreds of thousands of miles of gas (remember these are very big stars, 8 to 50 times larger than our sun!). And again if that shock wave were to completely stall, our unfolding saga, the progression of the complexity in the Universe would have ended right then and there, because none of the heavier elements past hydrogen or helium would have been dispersed out into the Universe to make planets and the next generation of stars.

But something barely credible happens. (The creativity of the Universe is not to be underestimated.) As cosmologists John Gibbon and Martin Rees delineate in their book "Cosmic Consequences" the neutrinos that have, up until that point, only been created in the earliest moment of the Universe's existence and released as part of the fusion process-these phantom neutrinos, (and they are phantoms, considering that they can travel through a million miles of lead without interacting with it at all) seem to have been created for no apparent reason. Well actually, come to find out, there was a reason: they add the necessary boost of energy to give the expanding shock wave in supernovas the extra push needed to completely blow the star apart (good Universal foresight).

This is how it happened and is still happening, for that matter. In a nutshell: back when the star's core was violently compressed by the incoming gas, when the core rebounded, a tremendous amount of neutrinos were generated and released as part of the energy of the rebound. The neutrinos then shoot out of the core at near the speed of light, but because the matter that comprises the wall of the incredibly dense gas is so thick, the neutrinos actually interact with it, helping it to reverse its direction and propel it along. This timely boost of intense energy compels the now expanding shock wave of elements and gas to forcefully continue on its way, leading to the dispersal of the star's contents into the surrounding space at extraordinarily-high velocities (Nothing to it. No problem!).

This is all interesting in its own right, and as always seems improbable to have happened, all things considered. But it is stranger than that, because the neutrinos only interact with matter through the weak force and then only extremely rarely. To make the point, billions of neutrinos have passed through you as you have read this sentence.

Here once again is an example of the necessary, but improbable, strength of a fundamental force of Nature coming into play. It was discovered that if the weak force is stronger by just a little bit, the neutrinos would stay locked up in the core of the imploding star and wouldn't escape. And again, if the weak force is slightly weaker, the neutrinos wouldn't interact with the matter comprising the shock wave either, they'd blow through without affecting it, and the shock wave isn't pushed forward and none of the heaviest elements wind up being created and dispersed in space. So the Universe once again would have just become a lifeless dud (same old story).

There are a few more interesting things about supernovas worth mentioning: they create the elements heavier than iron, elements with larger more complex nucleuses (elements like silver, gold and uranium). These elements are created by the high energy and heat in the interior of the star during the implosion and the rebound of the core, and in the neutrino-loaded-super-heated shock wave as it plows through the star. When large numbers of these newly created highly complex and unstable nucleuses go through radioactive decay (break apart), they produce so much energy that a supernova will (for a couple of weeks) shine as bright as the entire galaxies that contain them, with their billions of other stars. That calculates out to be the entire energy output of our very own sun in its almost 10 billion year life span. By the way, one or two go off per century in any given galaxy, and one every second in the Universe at large. And if a planet with any life forms is in the vicinity of one, that planet is basically sterilized. So, you can put that unsettling fact on your long list of things to worry about, but somewhere near the bottom I hope.

So now the Universe, with its long list of complex elements dispersed in space, is set to embark on the next phase of its unfolding. Evolution doesn't quite seem like the right word to use, even though it commonly is in cosmology, because there has been no competition for the survival of the fittest star, particle, or strength of force, for that matter. Electrons with different charges don't compete for nuclei. But, on the other hand, you'll remember matter did compete, in a way, with antimatter and won out (barely).

That being said the Universe needs some planets to go along with the stars, right? How does that advantageous event happen? (You guessed it. Next essay!)

TWELVE

THE FORMATION OF THE EARTH AND MOON

So, here we are in the early Universe. The stars have been exploding and their debris has been dispersed far and wide; space has been littered with dust and gas. If you think about it, that is actually quite a remarkable accomplishment for our little speck of red-hot space from way back when, at the literal beginning of time: that it had exploding things we now call stars. But, as usual, the Universe had yet another trick up its sleeve. Planets! And planets mean solar systems, with of course the question being: How did the Universe manage to pull that off?

The answer commences with dark matter. We should keep in mind that without this mysterious something and its consolidating effects there would be no galaxies or stars, because gravity, as we now know, surprisingly doesn't have enough strength to pull dispersing gas molecules back together to make stars, unless the gas is highly concentrated for some reason (such as the shock waves generated by supernovas for instance). Without our friend dark matter, the Universe's early gas would have just continued on its merry way unimpeded.

But "luckily" (there's that word again) with the help of the bewildering dark matter generating its gravitational effects, enormous pockets of concentrated gas did become over time, vast galactic like structures. These extremely large areas of dark matter must have had within them smaller regions where it was slightly more condensed; these areas facilitated the gaseous matter to form into stars, that over time would blow themselves up and reconfigure and blow themselves up again. This succession of supernovas created stars with progressively higher levels of complex elements.

By the way, stars come in different colors and sizes with varying live spans; most do not become supernovas and just fade away as brown dwarfs. Our sun will become a red giant and later a white dwarf that will gradually fade away; starting in about 5 billion years.

As just mentioned, because our sun wasn't big enough to quickly explode, there was time for our solar system to develop. This happened over time when a substantial area of concentrated gas and dust started coalescing into a vast swirling cloud, that gradually sped up as the bulk of the material within it flowed towards the central area (somewhat like a figure skater pulling their arms into their bodies to generate speed). This region of gas and dust gradually flattened out into a disk like formation, then steadily over millions of years the disk began to slow somewhat, in part because of the magnetic fields generated within it.

In this disk the greater part of the material (99.9 percent in fact) ended up in the central area and became our star; a third generation star in the case of our sun (It takes at least two generations of supernova explosions to generate the necessary levels of heavy elements to make rocky-metal-rich planets). The .1 percent of the material, which remained in the outer regions of the disk, slowly but increasingly became congealed into planets, moons, comets and asteroids.

These objects came about because of the fact that in the space of the forming disk, the free-floating elements combined with others to form different compounds (water being an example), with the aid of electrostatic forces acting upon them; after a while these elements and compounds started to bunch up (like dust balls). After they attained certain size gravity started pulling them into even larger clumps, and so it went until they reached planetesimal size conglomerations.

This process continued: bigger planetesimals sweeping up the smaller ones, along with any other left over debris, and fairly quickly (not really!) you have something resembling a planet emerging. The earth is still in the process of gathering up the remaining debris in its path and that debris can be seen as incoming meteorites (shooting stars) on a clear night, but can occasionally come in as a menacing, highly disruptive asteroid or comet.

When these asteroid type objects started slamming into each other the kinetic energy of their collisions was converted into heat, which allowed the ever-enlarging objects to start to melt and round out. After a certain planetary size was reached, the now heated-molten elements, being in a semi-fluid state, started to gather into layers with the heavier elements (iron, nickel and a host of radioactive ones) creating a more highly condensed and intensely hot core area.

Let's try not to take any of this highly improbable scenario for granted, and just skip over it while trying to have some vague understanding of the whole process. This is ridiculously complicated stuff we are talking about, with the entire array of forces fully in play that are "somehow"(you'll see I like this word too, like "luckily") intrinsic to this once spontaneously generated Universe of ours.

That being said, back to our story: in the case of the earth's orbital zone, as good fortune would have it, two such planet-sized objects were produced. Sooner or later they were bound to collide and when they finally did the fireworks went off in a spectacular fashion. When they collided (it was a substantial glancing blow not a direct hit) they basically exploded, with a lot of the aftermath ending up in orbit around the larger remaining remnant of the two. The larger remnant, which ended up being our very own earth, had been knocked on its side a little from the hit (23 degrees actually), and this whole violent episode surprisingly ends up being a "lucky" break for a variety of reasons. The one that most of us enjoy is seasonal change, which is due entirely to the earth's tilted axis, a relic from that billions-of-years-old violent encounter (how about that!).

The moon was congealed out of the orbiting wreckage of the collision. And that now still orbiting remnant of the collision has profound implications when it comes to the development of the conditions necessary for "advanced" life to have gradually arisen on the then-smoldering-inhospitable planet below. For one thing the earth's axis would have gone through dramatic oscillations without the moon stabilizing it. This would have all but prohibited the development of advanced life as we know it, because of the wild climate swings that would have inevitably taken place over time.

There are a number of interesting things about the moon worthy of note mentioned by Robert M. Hazen in his excellent book "The Story of Earth." One is that after the moon formed it was much closer to the earth than it is now. It was only 15,000 miles away and looked 16 times bigger than it looks to us today and it was also at least a 100 times brighter. The moon was geologically active then, with volcanoes and seas of molten magma pooling up in valleys (creating the man in the moon effect).

Also, the moon at that time, exerted tremendous tidal forces on the earth, pulling the earth's semi-molten surface almost a mile upward with every overhead passing. And the passes happened often, because the earth then had a 5-hour day. The moon itself went around the earth in about 3 or 4 days, with all this wild geological activity adding to the earth's internal heat.

That, by the way, was about 4.6 billion or so years ago. Now the moon is 239,000 miles from the earth and it takes 29 days to make a circuit. It continues to recede from the earth at the unhurried pace of about 1½ inches a year, as the earth's rotation also leisurely continues to slow.

Another point of interest (at least to me) is that at this particular point in time, the moon and the sun appear from our perspective to be basically the exact same size relative to each other (what are the odds of that?). This shows up in remarkable fashion during a lunar or solar eclipse when they fit directly on top of each other, even though the sun is 93 million miles away from us, and millions of times bigger than the moon.

Along the same line, there are times in the month when just as the full moon is rising in the east, the sun is setting in the west, and if you are in an expansive terrain to witness it, the timing is nearly perfect and it almost seems to have a philosophical significance. The implication perhaps being that this earth of ours offers moments of seeming perfection when things fall into place or alignment, but these are for the most part rare and generally short-lived. The inevitable wilt of a perfect flower is a common poetic example. That being the case, it seems to be a good idea to try and pause and appreciate these uncommon but special moments when they occur.

Now let's come back to earth from the moon. From any objective perspective, we could say that early on the earth didn't offer much promise, being a violent, inhospitable, steaming and molten sphere to begin with. And once again, there was no indication at all of the remarkable and interesting things to come. Certainly not anything even remotely resembling life seemed to be in the cards. How did we get to where we are today, an earth with life in all its abundance, from that hot mess? We will look at how this unexpected transformation took place in the up coming essays.

But first another quick aside, this occurrence of stars being created with planets around them is the norm thoughout the Universe. New planets orbiting around distant stars are being discovered almost daily, in all manner of sizes and configurations. The Universe in all probability must have trillions of planets orbiting stars in its billions of galaxies (That sentence would make Carl Sagan proud!).

THIRTEEN

MAKING THE EARTH HABITABLE

All the planets were, in retrospect, unlikely to develop into anything other than barren desolate wastelands or giant balls of gas. The phenomenon of life at the early stages in earth's existence didn't seem even like a remote possibility. We are all used to things that are alive, obviously ourselves included, but if you think about how unlikely that molten sphere we discussed in the previous essay would become the earth we experience today, from any objective perspective, it would seem to have been wildly improbable, to the point of impossible.

There were clearly a large number of events that had to take place before the earth could manifest itself and sustain life as we know it; we are talking now about advanced-complex organisms, not just the earliest bacterial-types of life forms (which are remarkable in themselves) that can exist in the most highly unlikely places. Life forms in this initial stage of development are probably a fairly common occurrence throughout the Universe—advanced life forms like your pet poodle much less so.

With our busy lives and preoccupations, we hardly ever take into consideration all the things that were needed to take place on the Earth to enable it to support creatures like us. It is a fairly remarkable list of highly unlikely events, from the perspective of this series of essays, providential in nature. See what you think.

Let's start in the center of the earth and work outward. The core consists of iron and nickel in a semi-liquid state. The core and the convection currents in the surrounding layers generate a magnetic field without which we don't exist. Why? Because these magnetic fields create lines of invisible force that deflect incoming solar winds comprised of deadly-highly-charged particles. These particles would extinguish any land-based life forms before they had any chance of developing. Life would have remained hidden and tucked away somewhere out of harm's way in the ocean.

The solar wind is not all bad, by the way; it was responsible for blowing out and away from the earth most of the hydrogen and helium that had accumulated around it. It was blown into the nether regions of the solar system to be collected by the now giant gaseous planets that were forming way out there at the time; another more aesthetically attractive benefit of these dangerous charged particles is that they are responsible nowadays for generating the shockingly beautiful northern lights.

Also in the core regions are large concentrations of heavy radioactive elements, created in those Supernova explosions we have discussed in other essays. These elements were and are generating heat in their breakup; kinetic heat left over from the incoming asteroids can be put into the heat generating mix. All of this accumulated heat is important because it's responsible for making geological processes on the surface of our planet possible to this day.

Those processes drive life-enhancing plate tectonics (to be discussed shortly), which are essential to the creation of large land masses, maintaining a relatively low salinity level in the world's oceans, recycling carbon dioxide back into the atmosphere, and as a bonus, aiding to the generation of biodiversity in the creation of multiple continents. Additionally, most significant theories of the origin of life itself, involve what takes place around or near the fissures in the crust that are produced in the movement of these large plates. Without all this crustal movement, life as we know it would have stalled out or possibly not developed at all, as we soon will see in upcoming essays.

How does all that massive, at one time unthinkable, continental movement happen? It wasn't until the 1970's that the existence of continental drift (plate tectonics) was confirmed. The idea itself had been around for a while and largely dismissed. It's a bit of a long story (but an interesting one) that we needn't get into, but after it was accepted as a fact, it ended up explaining a whole lot, if not most, of the geological features on the earth. Up until that point, mountain ranges, earthquakes, fossils of marine animals and marine mineral deposits in high elevations to name just a few, remained a complete mystery as to their origins.

Now we know the earth has 9 large plates (24 in all) moving in all different directions in relation to each other and they often collide. In fact they are colliding right now, and when they have a collision, the one with the heavier material (ocean floor basalt) goes under the other lighter plate made of granite (continental land masses) taking rock, saltwater, and heat from the friction of the grinding process with it. It also takes along with it heat-inducing carbon, in the form of calcium carbonate that makes up 50 percent of limestone, which is made from the skeletons of marine animals. An example of this limestone, by the way, is apparent in the beautiful white cliffs of Dover.

If the materials in the colliding plates have the same density, then there is a collision that generates a major upliftment, creating mountain ranges such as the Himalayas. The Himalayas were created when a relatively small plate (what is now known as India and the surrounding countries today) gradually pushed into the larger Asiatic plate. Because both were made of the lighter granite type rocks, they got into a major shoving contest. As a result of being equally matched, up went the Himalayas and they are still going up today.

Those mountains created there and elsewhere help facilitate the weathering process that also helps take carbon out of atmosphere. This is done when the carbon in the atmosphere couples with the available minerals on the mountainsides during rain and the snow's melting runoff. This process of weathering helps maintain the earth's temperature within a habitable range (again necessary for life's complexity to be sustained, at least on land).

In other places on earth, in the so-called subduction zones, the carbon locked up in the minerals in the plate being subducted gets heated up in the upper mantle and is recycled back into the atmosphere through volcanic eruptions, which are a common feature in those areas overlying subduction zones. One such area is the "ring of fire" found in the western Pacific, where the Pacific plate subducts under the Asiatic one, unfortunately taking slivers of Mexico (the Baja peninsula) and California with it. We should now be starting to get a sense of some of the balancing act that is taking place on this planet to maintain its atmosphere in a proper balance of gases for life's basic benefit.

Early on, incidentally, the earth was almost completely covered by water with just a few volcanoes dotting a massive trans-global ocean, with no continents. The granite that now forms the continents is lighter and floats on the heavier ocean floor basalt, and is created when the basalt is heated up at least twice (go figure). The reigning theory for the formation of the continents goes something like this: it starts with volcanoes being generated over upward-flowing convection currents of magma called hotspots. These areas double-heat the basalt to make continental granite (The Hawaiian islands being one example of a hot spot; there are several others). Some scientists speculate that asteroid impacts also generated enough heat to create pockets of granite.

After pockets of granite had come into existence, one way or another, the continents were gradually created over the subduction zones. This happened when the patches of granite scattered over the plates started accumulating like the sweeping of scattered debris into a pile before a dustpan.

Another thing that plate tectonics was essential for, besides making the continents, was keeping the world's oceans life-friendly and habitable. This is because water in the world's oceans gradually build-up high levels of salt, given that it is continually coming in from the land through the runoff of hundreds of rivers and streams. High levels of sodium in the oceans would make advanced life much harder to develop and continue to thrive. That's because of its tendency to draw water out of cell membranes (meat is salted to kill the bacteria in this way).

Fortunately, the seawater is recycled every 100,000 years or so through the subduction process. That's important because when the seawater is heated it loses most of its salt content through its mineralization. The subterranean water reenters the oceans through the mid-ocean fault lines that continually spew out molten lava and the salt-free water, creating new ocean floor in the process. As one example, this process is still spreading South America and Africa farther apart. Incidentally, the finding of these active fault lines that circle the globe like the stitches on a baseball played a major part in the acceptance and confirmation of the theory of plate tectonics,

In addition, the earth's place in the solar system, at large, plays into advanced life's eventual development too, in ways that you probably have not considered. One is that it is obviously closer to the sun than the giant gaseous outer planets, so the solar winds, as earlier mentioned, were powerful enough at this range to clear out the large, then enveloping atmosphere that had been accumulating.

Our planet also needs to be in a zone where water, in all three of its phases, can exist (liquid, solid and gas). But a much less-known fact is that without Jupiter (a thousand times larger than the earth and made mostly of gas) being out there doing us a favor by vacuuming up asteroids and water in the form of comets (earth's surface water comes from both the steam coming out of volcanoes and the early Earth's incoming comets and asteroids) the Earth would have been a much different place.

Starting with the fact that without most of the larger earth-threatening asteroids being swept up, there would have been many more mass extinctions, instead of the 5 or 6 that our planet has been subject to (don't stew too long on that grim fact). Advancing complex life would have been disrupted or stopped in its tracks much more often by those catastrophic-incoming-life-stifling explosions. (Mass extinctions aren't all bad, because the last one put the dinosaurs out of business leading to the rise of mammals, ourselves included.) It is hard to say how much more water would have been added to the amount that exists now on Earth without Jupiter's presence, but it would by most conservative estimates have made the Earth essentially and perhaps even today almost totally enveloped in water (Water World!). That fact would have had a profound affect on life's land based advancement. Dolphins or something like them would perhaps be the pinnacle in life's development at this point in time without Jupiter's benign influence.

So, those floating dispersed particles of gas and dust drifting in cold-empty space had a little magic in them didn't they? One was the earth, and one of the others is the magic we call life. That free-floating dust and gas was helped along and brought together by multiple forces with just the right amount of strength and affect. It is a totally implausible scenario, this long series of events we have just been through (along with the moon's stabilizing effect, of course), this making of stars and planets and what goes on inside and outside of them to enable us to be here.

But before we look at life's remarkable origin, let's look in the next essay at that extraordinary and mystifying, yet common element we usually take totally for granted: water.

FOURTEEN

WATER

If you are looking for something astonishing and amazing, go into the kitchen and turn on the faucet. What comes out, if your plumbing is functioning, is one of Nature's most unlikely, implausible and beneficial manifestations – water!

This usually taken-for-granted substance was originally created in cold-dark space with hydrogen and oxygen atoms adhering to grains of dust. Water is a classic, iconic really, example of an emergent-phase-transition; what this means is that as the Universe unfolds there are aspects of it that seemingly come out of nowhere. In emergent-phase-transitions there is nothing self-evident beforehand that indicates what is about to take place, it just spontaneously emerges as a revealed "hidden" quality of the unfolding Universe. And quite often in Nature, the whole ends up being greater than its parts (kind of like the Beatles). This happens repeatedly right down the line, from quarks to atoms, to molecules to minerals, to substances all the way up to the magic of consciousness in a web of cells in a brain, all with qualities not predictable until after their appearance.

Water makes this point, of improbable qualities emerging out of nowhere, as well as anything else found in Nature, in that this liquid consists of two gases. And what usually happens when you combine two gases? You get a third gas that is simply a combination of the two, like the nitrogen and the oxygen in our atmosphere, right? No, not always, Nature had something else in store for hydrogen and oxygen: they became water, a substance with extraordinary and unforeseeable qualities. And because of the affinity of the two atoms it consists of, along with their abundance in the Universe, it's a common molecule.

What happened with these two gases that allowed them to make such a remarkable substance? (Let's get just a little technical for a moment.) It's because of the laws and complexities of atomic structure, the way atoms can interact by sharing their electrons in their outer shells. In this case, the oxygen atom has the need for 2 extra electrons to complete its outer shell's quota; this enables it to attract 2 hydrogen atoms and these atoms easily bond together by this sharing of electrons (lucky, lucky). After the electrons are being shared in the outer orbitals, the resulting H2O molecules look vaguely like Mickey Mouse with his two big ears, because of the hydrogen atoms being oriented somewhat close together on one side of the oxygen atom. Fortunately, because of the positioning of the hydrogen atoms on one side (for very technical reasons), the inherent charges of the oxygen and hydrogen atoms don't cancel each other out completely and the water molecule is endowed with a positive and negative polar aspect to it.

Because the charges of the resulting polarity aren't particularly strong, the atoms in water can move freely about each other in loose-forming hydrogen bonds, giving water its fluidity (each atom is loosely bonded with four others at a time and they are always in motion). That being said, the bonds are strong enough to create a noticeable surface tension, generating the droplets we are all familiar with on wet surfaces, such as the dew on the grass in the morning. Small insects (water striders and some spiders, even a quick-water-walking lizard) take advantage of this fact to skim across the top of water surfaces. Perhaps as a kid you floated a pin by placing it carefully on the top of water; if you had looked closely, you would have seen the indentation that these pins made on the surface. This adhering quality inherent in water is an important fact; this surface tension, along with water's cohesive and adhesive qualities, is what facilitates the capillary action that takes place in plants, and in our bodies for that matter. Without the way water binds to itself and adheres to surfaces, plants couldn't draw water up to their heights against the force of gravity to transport the required nutrients necessary for their growth.

The bonding power of water is such that if you could string its individual molecules together they would dangle jointly for hundreds of feet. So in the case of a plant when one molecule of water evaporates in a leaf, it pulls another up to take its place.

Additionally, because of this capacity, water can be drawn out of the earth and is re-circulated in the atmosphere as a gas (water vapor) through evaporation. It is important to note that surprisingly, (at least I was surprised when I found out), all water should be a gas at room temperatures and should not exist on the earth in liquid form at all if it followed the example of comparable substances found in Nature (again, that quality is because of the hydrogen bonds).

The hydraulic cycle (that we are all familiar with), this cycling of water through the atmosphere back down into the ground, is easy to take for granted. But when living in semi-arid places, as a lot of us do, and if it is looked at objectively, it seems incredible that water can and does fall out of the sky.

Anyway, let's look at some more of the remarkable (and fortunate for us) characteristics of water. For a start, it's transparent (also odorless, tasteless and has a neutral PH value, along with low electrical conductivity when in a pure uncontaminated state). Other liquids are cloudy or opaque. This fact gives all the obvious advantages of the possibility of vision and photosynthesis being developed in the advancing life forms (particularly complex life) that evolved within it. Think for a moment how different the world would be if water wasn't transparent.

Also, water is almost a universal solvent because of the polarity discussed previously. With its polarity it can pull other substances apart enabling them to mingle and mix within the active water molecules. These circulating substances can join up with whatever else they find more attractive, whether it is something dissolved in water or perhaps an attractive surface area it finds itself on. This was certainly the case for the substances that were needed to be brought together to assist in the initial development of the early forms of life on our planet. Life and almost all biological processes within it are without exception almost inconceivable without water.

The list goes on and on, with up to "seventy" anomalies of water compared to other liquids, but one of the most important aspects of water on these lists, concerning life, is that water in its solid form (ice) doesn't sink into itself when it freezes. This is due to how it becomes molecularly aligned when frozen, developing its attractive crystalline like structures. This fact actually makes water become less dense when it freezes and not more, so frozen water floats in itself. This is a peculiar quality, again, when we compare it to all other liquids; other frozen liquids become denser and sink into themselves.

Imagine for a moment if ice was denser than liquid water and did sink. Surface water would continue to freeze and drop down to the bottom in winter until the entire body of water would become rock solid from its bottom to top. Complex life, as we know it, would not have had much of an opportunity to develop. The bulk of the Earth's oceans would basically be just a block of ice with only spots of liquid water around fissures and volcanic cones here and there. Equatorial regions would have liquid water, but this would probably not have given much of an opportunity for any but the most rudimentary life forms to have developed.

Here are just a couple of more of the many things worth mentioning about water's beneficial aspects concerning life on land. Without its strong surface tension, raindrops couldn't develop, as has been mentioned, and there would at best perhaps just be a foggy-type mist in the air. And, of course, with water the way it is, when these condensed water droplets are large enough they fall to earth and seep into the cracks and crevasses of rocks all over the planet. And when the water freezes it expands (as only it does) and eventually breaks the rocks up into soil, along with the erosive effects of flowing water and wind in more temperate regions. And without soil, where would we be? Well, we plainly would not be here.

Thankfully, water is what it is, and we can appreciate the fact that the Universe manifested itself as a whole lot of it. And a little of it became you and me, actually a major part of you and me, something like seventy percent of us.

In the next essay we will look at some of the possible origins of the life that managed to somehow develop and take place within this atypical, life-facilitating substance we need and enjoy.

FIFTEEN

LIFE'S ORIGIN

Besides the origin of the Universe itself, for my money the origin of life comes in as a close second as far as mysteries go. The fact that there is anything even remotely resembling life (self-replicating animated matter) in the Universe is almost incomprehensible from what we have learned about the Universe's previous stages of development (quarks, protons, exploding stars, just to re-mention a few). To belabor the point, take a look around you and think that all that you see and the body your consciousness inhabits was, a little over 4 ½ billion years ago, gas and dusk floating in unimaginably cold dark space. I don't care if you leave that gas and dust to its own devices for a 100 billion years, it shouldn't become us. From any detached-objective perspective what we are experiencing right now is astonishing, if you put yourself in the right state of mind. That being said, we are now going to leave that state of mind and see what science has to say about this profound mystery.

One way some scientists look at life is an advanced form of chemistry (chemists of course). They consider its beginnings to have taken place when highly developed molecules had randomly come together and started being able to replicate themselves (nothing unusual about that!). These molecules must have been in places where the chemicals and energy needed for their creation, and later replication, were in abundance, or at least flowing through. The spaces are necessarily limited due to the fact that there had to be at least a certain level of sustained concentrations of the minerals and molecules that were necessary and indispensable in generating and maintaining the continued replication of these earliest forms of life. Otherwise the whole process would have just stalled out, and perhaps many times it did.

These life ingredients, so to speak, needed energy from some source (to emulate early metabolism) to facilitate their initial replication processes. Without energy added to the arrangement of substances, nothing would or could have happened. The necessary energy was not in short supply; the early earth had plenty of it in places. Also the inherent energy of the molecules themselves, after they had been drawn together by molecular forces, could have played a vital role, as they do today. Sunlight, as once thought, may not be as necessary or important as it was once considered to be.

Interestingly, comets and meteorites were still pulverizing the earth in large numbers at the first detectable point of life's presence. This leads many to believe that early life forms must have been tucked away in some reasonably protected environments, somewhere in the ocean's depths no doubt. Scientists, by the way, have made these points in time determinations of life's early development, using a wide variety of sophisticated methods (such as analyzing the geological time signatures of the rocks the earliest biological fossils have been found in).

It is now believed, as noted in a previous essay, that the earth at that early point in its existence was covered with a deep primordial coating of water, and the atmosphere and ocean had a heavy carbon dioxide content (the precise composition of the early atmosphere and ocean are continually going through revisions). So the delicate molecular life forms, at the start, were vulnerable to being extinguished even before they had time to get started, by this barrage of incoming space debris. But somehow life remarkably did get started, and it managed to survive and flourish. It's possible, if not probable, that life had many starts and stops in multiple places before it was securely established. We don't know, and can never be exactly sure where life was first established, but what we do know is that existing life had just "one" surviving starting point, as genetic evidence shows, and that one initial speck of fragile molecular life leads all the way to us and every other living organism.

The ingredients of life: minerals, compounds, amino acids and lipids (fats), are in the process of being recreated by scientists in laboratory experiments worldwide. These experiments emulate the conditions that scientists regard as possibly prevalent four or so billion years ago on our planet.

They have occasionally been successful in creating some of life's original building blocks (amino acids for example). Intriguingly, meteorites have also been found to have some of the same necessary ingredients that are part of life's early make up. So whether already here on earth or delivered from space, or both, the Universe in general, we can assume, abounds with what is required to get life started. So if life somehow started to flourish here in such inhospitable conditions, it seems highly probable that in at least in its more rudimentary and primitive forms, it is a fairly common occurrence throughout the Universe (advanced forms of life are a completely different story). But is there any clue as to where the most probable incubator for getting life started existed? Maybe!

Nick Lane in his engaging book "The Vital Question" offers a cogent and convincing scenario. Here are some of the main lines of reasoning and evidence brought forth. The geologically active areas "near" the plate-driving oceanic fissures that contain alkaline vents are presented to be the one of the most feasible candidates for life's early beginnings. These fairly mild alkaline vents found near the fissures, as opposed to the red-hot, black-smoky vents found directly above the fissures, have recently started to win favor.

For a while, the black smoking vents were considered by many as the most likely candidates for life's early development, when they were found to be teeming with life after their fairly recent discovery. It was surprisingly discovered that these vent-oriented life forms could exist without sunlight, by geological processes alone. About the same time, it was also revealed that bacterial life forms could exist in incredibly harsh conditions, such as near-boiling water and fairly extreme acidic environments. These emerging facts initially helped (still do) the case being made for the extreme, some say hellish, environments directly adjacent to the mid-ocean lava spewing vents as possibly being a site of life's early advent.

You may remember, as I do, the time when nice, tropical, sunlit coves (the blue lagoon) were where life was supposed to have emerged on the gentle accommodating earth (Darwin himself like this scenario). It is a pleasant idea, but that idyllic belief hasn't really panned-out. The bottom line is, we just don't know for sure. Scientists are looking at possibilities and probabilities. That being said, one of the most promising possibilities are the alkaline vents that Nick Lane advocates, for a number of reasons.

The alkaline vents we are talking about (life generally favors alkaline environments) look like giant, undersea termite mounds. These mound-like structures are found a few miles from the more toxic, extremely hot, so-called black smokers above the fissures mentioned earlier. There are a number of reasons they are looked upon favorably as a possible site of life's early origin. For one, they have small cell-sized pockets loaded with the right types of molecules that are in dynamic exchange with the surrounding ocean waters. Most importantly, they have an available flow of hydrogen seeping up out of the ocean floor – this detail is highly important. It is a little known fact, but an extraordinarily important fact, that "all life" uses the flow of hydrogen (ion proton gradients) within its cells to generate energy (we'll delve into this amazing process in coming essays).

But even with all the necessary ingredients in place, it is an astonishingly big jump from lifeless matter to even the simplest organisms. We have no fossil record of this unlikely transformative process, and it remains a profound and deep mystery exactly how it happened. All we can do is develop logical scenarios and try to duplicate them in the laboratory, with none having been successful so far.

When we finally can pick up the thread of what happened in the fossil record, the cells that are already present have surprisingly complex metabolic and reproductive capacities. These primitive bacteria-like cells have the astonishingly remarkable adaptive capability of invading and accommodating to virtually every available nook and cranny on the earth. Bacteria are now found from the upper stratosphere on dust to miles below the earth's surface. Life is shockingly durable, resilient and adaptive.

Life, after gaining its foothold stayed, in its simple prokaryotic (without a nucleus) form for billions of years. Then there came an abrupt transformation, a surge of different more-advanced life forms, the so-called Cambrian explosion. This bewildering event is when the more complex multi-cellular organisms, with nucleuses (eukaryotes), made astonishingly rapid (geologically speaking) advances in the complexity and diversity of their forms. This took place about 460 million years ago.

Interestingly, as with the prokaryotic cells, all of the eukaryotes or complex cells also come from just one genetic line. This line of cells enhanced its internal energy supply by one of its original members assimilating another smaller bacteria. These bacteria that were assimilated (eaten but not digested) became the mitochondria and chloroplasts that are now pervasive within cells. These energy-creating stations are absolutely necessary for a cell's more complex functions to take place and for advanced plants and animals to be maintained. Without this symbiotic relationship, complexity, as we know it, could not have happened. Also the higher levels of oxygen in this era generated by the chloroplasts themselves, seems to have been a key component in this rapid expansion of life's diversity of forms.

It was by these simple bacteria-like cells (now the chloroplasts within cells) devising the remarkably ability to break up water molecules by using sunlight that started changing the content of the atmosphere, to the one just mentioned with much higher levels of oxygen. This process took millions of years, and it is noteworthy that to begin with oxygen was highly toxic to life (still is to certain living organisms). But oxygen only remained a toxin for a while; life evolved accommodations to its lethal effects. In the long run, these revolutionary accommodations enabled ever-higher levels of metabolic activity, and this higher level of metabolic activity allowed larger animals to evolve.

So if we step back a bit and look dispassionately at life's unlikely occurrence, it is hard to imagine the Universe's ability to manifest itself as life as some random event; produced by a wildly improbable series of lucky happenstance springing spontaneously into existence and developing from what we have been considering. Life is astonishing in its complexity even in its simplest forms, as we will later explore, and it is far more reasonable to think of it as another "emergent property," a quality of the Universe that was waiting to manifest itself (like so many others) from the very beginning, in the same way as electrons, atoms and planets, emerged when conditions allowed them to appear, as opposed to the idea of life as an end-result of some radical series of chance flukes generated by dumb luck.

This unlikely event called life has many extraordinary aspects (everything about it really), but perhaps the most amazing is DNA, along with the RNA that is considered to have come before it. These two miraculous molecules are the blueprint and the providers in cells that enable them to replicate a complete organism through biologically encoded information in a bewildering series of steps.

And just as surprising, in a way, is DNA's extraordinary capacity to repair itself and the consequences of mutations when it is not properly repaired. These mutations usually lead to some new unwanted development that is quickly winnowed out of the genome (this is the point in time when evolution as we usually think about it finally starts to come into play), but sometimes, amazingly, mutations produce an as yet un-manifested, advantageous quality that enables the organism to better adapt to its changing environment. What are the odds of that happening?

DNA and RNA are really quite remarkable. Let's look more closely at them in the next couple of essays.

SIXTEEN

DNA AND ITS REPAIR

After the Universe had sprung into existence, it seems to have had an objective: to manifest itself in progressive levels of complexity. And when it comes to complexity, what goes on in the realm of microbiology is almost beyond belief. It is astonishing, a far cry from those simplistic diagrams of cells we saw in school in hygone years. In the next few essays we will take a look at some of the things occurring at the molecular-biological level. It is a truly amazing realm of fast-moving, hidden-from-us events, bordering on what should be considered miraculous or at least wildly implausible. On this minute level the processes being enacted are staggeringly intricate and, until relatively recently, only vaguely known to exist (there were only limited hints). Let's start with a brief, cursory look at DNA and its repair.

DNA is the most complex molecule we find in the natural world; there is really nothing quite like it. It is a biological code that has come into existence in a series of steps that remain shrouded in mystery, in a period of time with no discernable fossilized record. We only have clues and speculative scenarios as to how it came into being. It is fairly safe to assume that the Universe must have started out with DNA, or something close to it, as an intrinsic, inherent probability that would come into existence when conditions would permit it to (a re-occurring theme). It is just too much to consider it a chance occurrence when you see how it operates along with its RNA counterpart. The Universe was made for life, it would seem, and life needs to replicate itself; that means something like DNA is necessary.

DNA is a remarkably complex molecule that contains the information or code necessary to make living organisms (how incredible is that!). Many of us have seen DNA's double helix represented as a gently twisting ladder-like structure. This helix has 2 outer spines of lined-up phosphate and sugar-type molecules, with an inner-connecting area made up of nitrogen-based molecules. These connecting molecules (rungs of the ladder) are called bases and there are 4 different types; they are the parts of the DNA molecule responsible for the coding of biological information. The 4 bases can be abbreviated as: A (adenine), T (thymine), C (cytosine), G (guanine); A and T always pair up across the helix, and the same goes for C and G. The coded information of these bases comes in groups of 3s, called codons; they are a little like three-letter words that when strung together become a long informative sentence. In this context, what these combinations of short words denote are proteins: the building blocks of life.

This will be a barebones, simplistic, quick look at how DNA's double helix duplicates itself, just to give you a general idea. To start the process off, the double helix is unzipped by enzymes, then special proteins move in and attach themselves to the now separated strands, keeping the strands from recombining. After that, nucleotides (the building blocks of DNA and RNA) are shuttled in by enzymes to connect with the existing bases of the two now separate chains of the DNA molecule (around 50 per second!). Subsequently, when all the nucleotide bases are connected to the corresponding bases (A to C and T to G), two newly minted complete DNA strands exist that will go into their own separate cells. By the way, at the end of the replication process, other enzymes look for mismatches in the DNA code that has now been recreated; if they find any, they replace the errors with the right nucleotides. If they don't complete this process successfully errors are passed on, and these errors could be catastrophic for the organism.

DNA is in the business of making proteins and there are hundreds of thousands of different kinds of proteins found in Nature, with more than 90 thousand different types to be found in the human body alone. DNA, being just the code, needs and uses RNA molecules to build all these different types of proteins. This is done in the cytoplasm, outside of the nucleus where the DNA molecule resides. This manufacturing of proteins is a bizarre and fascinating process that is so incredible that it is hard to believe it is actually going on in our cells (I'm not exaggerating here, it is ridiculously complicated). We will take a closer look at this extraordinary process in the following essay.

This obviously isn't a biology textbook and there is a whole lot else going on concerning DNA and its replication that we won't get bogged down with now (please watch one of the many videos available), but there are a few things worth mentioning about DNA in passing.

The DNA molecule is 6 billion base pairs long and takes a couple of hours to replicate. Each cell has a tangled-up dense ball of DNA in its nucleus (actually the DNA is lightly spooled around protein structures called histones). If you unraveled a strand, it would be about 6 feet long. Most of the DNA molecule seems to be nonfunctioning and is just reproduced without it having any, as yet, known affect on the organism (expect this to change as more research is done). In humans the DNA is packaged in 46 chromosomes that are made into 23 pairs, which only become evident just before cell division takes place. There are about 20 to 25 thousand genes that are the active parts of the so-called genome that reside in the chromosomes; some of these genes can be dynamic or passive depending on environmental influences (this is a fairly new discovery called epigenetics; it is helping explain many of our psychological and physiological functions). And here's a shocker: if all the DNA of our approximately 50 trillion cells (give or take a few trillion) were lined up, it would extend to the sun (93 million miles away, remember?) and back about 600 times or around the earth 5 million times (I love the people that figure this kind of stuff out!). That's probably enough facts, but it should give you some idea of the level of intricacy and complexity that emerged out of those gas and dust molecules floating freely in cold dark space a few billion years beforehand.

Things can go wrong (there's a surprise!) in the extravagant replication process we briefly touched on, or in the cell's completed DNA strands for a variety of reasons: solar radiation and chemicals are a couple of examples; there are many more. What's astonishing is that there are enzymes that sense these errors and extract the nucleotide bases that are inaccurate and through at least 5 different known processes replace the faulty bases with the right ones. Think about that for a moment. "Enzymes" somehow are making calls on what should be in place on the DNA chain; if they don't like what they find, they splice it out in an elaborate procedure and put the right nucleotide base or sequence of bases in its place. There are teams of these molecules working together, at breakneck speed, to pull all this off and they have to "evaluate" in some fashion over 6 billion of these base pairs in about two hours in the replication process and continually in the cell's functioning DNA. It sounds impossible doesn't it? How long do you think would it take you and me to go through and check 6 billion bits of information and replace the faulty bits (the equivalence of 10,000 books of 1,000 pages)? And they are all zipping around of their own accord "somehow" (I have never read a good explanation as to how they move around). We need to give a little credit to those tireless, mindless molecules working non-stop 24/7 for us in our cells to keep us alive.

Here is an important point that I have personally never heard considered or discussed. When scientists talk about how random mutations generate adaptive changes in an organism, they never mention how strikingly odd it is that an error in the code can lead to something adaptive that has never before existed. "Every aspect" of biology seems to have happened in this way (potential advantages coming from errors produced in the code).

For example, let's hypothetically take a gamma ray from some distant star hitting a gene that codes for the hair color brown. The gamma ray alters the sequence in the bases in the codon, and from something old (brown hair) comes something new (white hair). So on some level white hair, and everything else we find in life forms for that matter, was always "there" as a latent unrealized potentiality (it had to be). When these different base pairs in the biological code were put into a different arrangement, for whatever reason, a new hidden potential is realized and it continues to be expressed if environmental conditions favored it (the Arctic regions covered with snow, in this brown-to-white hair example).

So again, we could look at all evolutionary advances as latent possibilities that were always lurking on some hidden inherent level in the code, so to speak, waiting for the right opportunity to be expressed or manifested. It seems to be like so many other things (DNA included), once again, an emergent quality that came into existence in the Universe's unfolding when the opportunity presented itself.

As has been mentioned, DNA is "just" the code or the blue print of what needs to be created. RNA makes it come alive. Let's look at how it does that in the next essay.

SEVENTEEN

RNA AND RIBOSOME PROTEIN SYNTHESIS

The general consensus in the scientific community at this point in time is that RNA came before DNA. From this perspective, DNA is just the code developed by RNA to replicate itself-which is exactly the case. RNA is where all the magic happens. So somehow in an early earth environment a slice of RNA was improbably constructed and became actualized with the life-potential quality of reproducing itself. It also later ended up having the added value of being an enzyme (a molecule, usually a protein, able to speed up reactions between other molecules without being altered itself). And remarkably, somehow RNA developed the capacity to generate the ultra-complex, but basically inert, DNA double helix molecule to insure its continued reproduction. So it is not surprising that the puzzling RNA molecule and its derivatives remain the major factor in inner-cellular processes today.

It is safe to say, in my opinion, that the manufacturing of proteins within cells is one of the most astounding things to be found in Nature. The proverbial hidden hand of Spirit can be considered revealed here if you look at the process we are about to discuss from a spiritual perspective, of course. Scientists quite often don't see it that way, but it is such a remarkable process that it begs for an open-minded evaluation of its probability of developing through some sort of Darwinian type evolutionary pressure alone. So let's describe in some detail this remarkable process going on inside of every cell in our bodies at this very moment, the creation of proteins, and see what you think.

To start with, an enzyme is made aware "somehow" that a certain protein is needed for a specific purpose within our bodies. So this enzyme "holds" that information and shows up at the DNA molecule (moving on its own power in some way) and starts evaluating the DNA molecule (all six feet of it) to determines where the coded information for that particular protein is found. Remember there are 6 billion base pairs to sort through – 200 phonebooks worth of code to process to find the equivalence of a page worth of the right slice of genetic code to be used in that particular protein's construction.

The enzyme, after finding the right spot, unzips the DNA's double helix and then other industrious molecules start bringing in the bases necessary to construct a duplicate of that specific segment of DNA, which becomes the so-called messenger RNA (mRNA). This strand of mRNA will be used as a template to assemble the protein later on outside the nucleus in the cell's cytoplasm.

After the mRNA has been created from the DNA, a new set of clever "molecules" shows up and take out any sections of its code that won't be used (how could they possible know which part of the code will not be used?) Then the molecules splice the mRNA back together, as an old-fashion movie editor would have done to a film. Now the mRNA is at last ready to be on its way to make a protein.

At this point the mRNA literally snakes towards one of the many pores in the membrane surrounding the nucleus and exits into the cell's cytoplasm (how does it find the pore opening and how does the mRNA create the motion necessary to travel about?). After it has moved into the cytoplasm, a part of a ribosome (the protein-manufacturing center) to be used to produce the protein links up with it.

The ribosomes come in two parts, one smaller than the other. These two parts only connect when the mRNA (the code) has found and attached itself to the smaller unit. After that has happened, the bigger half senses ("somehow") the connection has been made between the mRNA and its smaller half, so it moves in and couples up with it and the process of manufacturing proteins begins.

We need to take into consideration that all this is taking place at an incredible rate of speed and that in the average mammalian cell there are over 10 million ribosomes toiling away making proteins at any given moment.

Now the smaller section starts moving the mRNA along while the larger half helps organize the arrival of the amino acids that are coming in at about 200 a minute. These amino acids are added on to the rapidly developing chain of other amino acids that have already been put together from the coded information in the mRNA; these chains of amino acids will become a protein. The average protein has about 250 amino acids linked up, but some proteins can be as long as 34,000 thousand amino acids in length.

These amino acids are being brought into place by another type of RNA molecule, this one being a molecule that transfers the amino acids into the ribosome; hence the name transfer RNA (tRNA). These tRNAs have the power, as all the others, to move about and sense where to go with their payloads ("again somehow"). I know, I know, I'm overdoing it with this "somehow" stuff. Actually, we can assume they are following some sort of biochemical signatures found in the cell's cytoplasm. How all these different types of RNA do all these things will be understood some day, but that doesn't make the processes we are talking about any less improbable and impressive.

Moving along. There are different tRNAs, one for each of the 20 various amino acids that are necessary to construct proteins. These tRNAs have as part of their makeup what is called an anticodon (3 nucleotides or bases lined up). These 3 bases on the anticodons connect with 3 complimentary bases on the mRNA molecule. When they attach themselves to the mRNA, their payload of an amino acid is connected to the amino acid that is already in place on the protein chain being created inside the ribosome.

Because the amino acids that have now been put into place bond more strongly with the adjacent amino acid in the chain than with the tRNA that brought them in, the tRNA can disconnect and slip away to find another free-floating amino acid in the cytoplasm to repeat the process again and again and again. You can, and really should, check out on Youtube, videos of all these things visually; talented people have made remarkable representations of most of these extraordinary processes.

By the way, the mRNA has a start and stop codon which is part of the information it encoded from the strand of unzipped DNA at the beginning of the sequence. Once the stop codon is reached, the process comes to an end and the strand of newly minted protein coils up through molecular forces and assumes the 3 dimensional structure that is vital for its intended function. The ribosome then separates its 2 halves, and either they dissolve or almost immediately go through the whole process again, while the newly minted proteins are off being transported to where they are needed.

So to beat the old drum, how does something like this bizarre and remarkable process "evolve" out of gas and dust, and later on out of a barren sterile earth? It would seem that unless these types of processes were not somehow (and that is a big unknown somehow) imbedded in the fabric of the Universe as hidden-intrinsic potentialities, they would have had no chance at all of developing or evolving.

That is not to say that the initial process that comes into existence cannot be refined by selective evolutionary pressure (which is probably the case), it's just how did they come into existence in the first place to be selected upon over time?

EIGHTEEN

PHOTOSYNTHESIS AND OXYGEN

Let's keep examining the microbiological world and its implausible occurrences. Most of us learned a little about photosynthesis in science class: how plants take in carbon dioxide and water and with the help of a little sunshine make carbohydrates, primarily in the form of sugars. We also probably learned that the oxygen we breathe is a by-product of the process. It seemed straightforward enough. With not much complexity involved as far as we could tell, there was really nothing to it. Guess what. We were wrong!

Let's go way back and take another look at early life forms. Cyanobacteria by some unknown means developed the ability to employ, to their advantage, simple molecules that respond to sunlight; these chlorophyll like molecules surprisingly could retain the excitation they received when they were hit by photons. These excitable molecules are the cornerstones of the photosynthetic process taking place in the chloroplasts found in plants. It should be remembered these chloroplasts now embedded in cells, at one time were free-living organisms. Billions of years ago, one of them was consumed by a larger bacterial cell but managed to survive digestion and developed a symbiotic (mutually beneficial) relationship with the devouring cell. Chloroplasts can still move around to reorient themselves to maintain some semblance of independence within the cell; they move to adjust to the amount of sunlight they want to absorb. They also still retain most of their own DNA.

It took time for photosynthetic organisms to become abundant, as indicated by the slowly but steadily rising oxygen levels evident in the fossil record. But being able to use sunlight to enhance their cell functions allowed them to flourish.

We can't do justice to the remarkable process of photosynthesis, even in a fairly nontechnical way, but let's just sketch out some notable basics about how photosynthesis works.

To start, the incoming photons strike the excitable chlorophyll molecules and this generates resonance (vibrational) energy; this energy in the form of agitated electrons is transmitted through a series of molecular structures in what, not unpredictably, is called an electron transport chain. This chain of events happens through protein structures and enzymes found in the chloroplast's membrane.

This transport chain is responsible for various things occurring; initially, it breaks up water molecules. This is the part of this complicated series of events that frees oxygen to be defused into the atmosphere along with something just as important: it frees protons (hydrogen ions), to be used later on in the second phase of photosynthesis to create complex carbohydrates.

A transport enzyme, in moving the exited electrons along, picks up protons from the surrounding fluid; these are the protons that have been freed and left in the cell's cytoplasm from the break-up of water. A number of processes within the stations or molecular structures in the chain deposit protons on the other side of a membrane in the cell in which the stations are located. This movement of the protons through the membrane creates what is called a proton-ion gradient (the force generated by two different electrical charges being on opposite sides of the membrane).

This gradient ends up being absolutely necessary for life, not just in plants but in all cells, because it supplies the energy required to manufacture life's workhorse, the ATP molecule (to be discussed in depth in the next essay). These ATP molecules are needed for all the cells multifarious metabolic functions, and I mean all of them!

At the end of the line, the electrons that have been moving through the chain help create a molecule called NADPH, and with its electrical potential, along with ATP, facilitate what is called the Calvin Cycle. This cycle (chemists put it up on their office walls as a thing of beauty) is remarkably complicated, but simply put, it is a series of reactions helped by the recently charged-up ATP and NADPH molecules that combine separate carbon-based molecules to make one carbohydrate or sugar molecule after a few metaphorical turns of the cycle (it is as convoluted as it sounds).

It's easier to understand when you see pictorial representations of the whole process, or better yet videos. In any case, that is generally speaking how photosynthesis makes oxygen and later in the process the precursor glucose that combines with other molecules to make lipids (fats), starches and other complex carbohydrates (food for plants themselves and us). So this process, simply put, is where the oxygen that was originally a toxin to the early forms of life, and later ended up being a necessity to life's later complex development, came from.

Through this vague sketchy overview, you should hopefully get the idea that this electron transport chain and what it accomplishes is once again a baffling process to have evolved out of dusty space. We can assume it evolved over time through multiple steps: the electron chain and the Calvin cycle. That being said, it seems to be yet another emergent quality inherent in the fabric of the Universe, destined to become manifest and refined when the conditions permit it to be. Where were the selective pressures to get this whole thing started from solely an evolutionary perspective?

Let's give oxygen its due:

An unexpected hidden bonus quality of this freed up oxygen is that it scoured and cleaned the air, way back when, helping to make it clear. It also cleared the early ocean waters of iron and magnesium by oxidizing them. After being oxidized, these elements fell to the bottom of the ocean floor to produce the red sediments which after hundreds of millions of years were uplifted to produce the geological bands that we occasionally see on the sides of mountains or along roadsides today.

Another extremely important aspect of what the would-be-toxin oxygen does, is to create the ozone level. That, along with the magnetic force lines generated by the earth's core, prevents the high-energy rays and particles coming from the sun from completely disrupting or destroying any DNA molecules they reach. That clearly would have slowed or prevented advance forms of life from developing, on land at least.

A surprising and unexpected thing about oxygen is that the oceans only exist because of the aforementioned core induced magnetic field and the oxygen-generated ozone level in the atmosphere. Without either, the radiation would have been so intense coming into the earth from the sun that the water molecules would have, early on, been gradually broken apart. The free oxygen being made available would have then readily forged chemical bonds with the earth's crustal rocks, which over time would have weathered it out of the atmosphere and deposited it into geological sediments. The freed hydrogen molecules in the break-up of water, would have eventually escaped into space and the oceans would have slowly but surely dried up and ceased to exist, as is the case on Venus and Mars.

Thankfully the wildly complicated process of photosynthesis came into being on our planet when it did, along with its toxic, but highly valuable byproduct oxygen. Once again, who could have imagined any of that coming from molecules floating freely in space?

NINETEEN

ATP AND THE ATP SYNTHASES

I have mentioned in a previous essay that scientists can trace back, by a variety of different methods, to only one cell line being the last-universal-common ancestor (LUCA) of all the forms of life found on our planet. So if life developed in multiple places on the ancient earth, it got extinguished one way or another.

At the time this surviving cell line was gaining a foothold leading to total dominance, a profound mystery lies as to how most of its basic features came into existence. It is unlikely there will be some sort of persuasive experimental evidence (fossils aren't available) to move towards any sort of general agreement as to how life developed its basic attributes. (It is a very long way from replicating RNA molecules to even the simplest forms of bacterial life with all of their complex organelles.) There are a whole host of mysteries concerning life's origin and later complexities, which are shrouded in the distant past waiting to be solved, and it is possible, if not probable, most of these questions will never be made clear.

You may remember, we talked about the possibility of life having been started in the alkaline vents because of the hydrogen that seeps out of the mantel in those particular areas. Hydrogen, as we know, has a single proton that surprisingly turned out to be the essential driver in the production of the ATP molecule, which is fundamentally important to all life. Let's take a deeper look into what ATP is and how it works its biological magic.

As just mentioned, ATP (adenosine triphosphate) is the source of all the energy that is used by life in virtually all its functions and processes. It has been said allegorically to be the money in the cell's economy. Nothing happens in live organisms without it. And get this: every cell in your body is consuming 10 million ATP molecules a second. With the body's estimated 40 to 50 trillion cells all engaged in the same process, you consume roughly your own weight in ATP daily. (Who knew!)

ATP is made (minted really) by molecular "machines" that are embedded in internal cell membranes, and to say a machine is not much of an exaggeration. This inconceivably small nano-manufacturing device has a number of parts that for all practical purposes, incredibly, look and act like a rotary motor. There are millions of these embedded in the thousands of mitochondria or chloroplasts located in any given cell, frenetically spinning out ATP molecules.

We will remember that mitochondria, like chloroplasts, were at one time bacteria that were enveloped to be dissolved and assimilated (eaten) by a larger cell, but both were co-opted instead to serve as an energy resource when their dissolution didn't take place. After a while the mitochondria and chloroplasts transferred most of their genes to the DNA of the host cell and now only a remnant remains in the mitochondria and chloroplasts themselves. (This remarkable type of gene transfer is a characteristic of bacteria and a fairly common occurrence.) Because the ATP synthases (the molecular machines mentioned above) are located in mitochondria and chloroplasts, they are both rightfully called the power stations of cells. These minute power stations produce their power by having the rotating turbines embedded in their membranes manufacture, or more precisely recharge, new ATP from used ADP (adenosine diphosphate) molecules. These small manufacturing turbines are powered by the proton-generated electrical gradient within the mitochondria and chloroplasts we have previously only touched upon.

The following is a brief description of how this remarkable manufacturing process works in animals. It all starts with electrons taken from the molecular remnants of food an animal ingests. This is the start of the process we know as cellular respiration. These electrons are passed down a chain of protein complexes, similar to what occurs in photosynthesis. At most stations in the electron chain, the electrons pull protons though the station and the protons end up on the other side of the folded membranes inside the mitochondria.

There are four of these stations in the chain and three of them directly place protons on the other side of the membrane. There are molecules, enzymes and proteins that transport electrons along this chain of molecular stations. This process is very similar to photosynthesis, in that from different starting points they basically achieve the same results – the now familiar to us proton-charged electrical gradient.

When this power being generated by the electrical gradient was first discovered and when it was realized how important it was to all biological processes, it was like a bolt out of the blue; it came as a complete surprise. Some say it ranks up there with the discovery of the theory of evolution. That's a bit of a stretch, but this gradient ends up being the primary driving force behind all life and no one knew about it until relatively recently.

The ATP synthase works because going through it is the only way the protons have of getting back through the cell membrane to relieve the pressure generated by their high concentrations on just one of its membrane's sides. But before we consider this flow of protons, somewhat like water through a grinding mill or a turbine in a dam that generates electrical power, let's take a closer look at the ATP synthase itself.

Where the protons enters the synthase is a rotor head that spins a little with each proton swiftly passing through it, with the protons being pulled along by the opposite negative electrical charge on the other side of the membrane we've talked about. There are about ten places for these incoming protons to reside as they briskly move through the synthase. The rotor head is connected to a shaft that drops down through the cell membrane to a separate, but connected, part of the synthase that is made up of six separate molecular conglomerations or bundles (look up a video or a diagram to help visualize it). By the way, there is a stator (a rod-like supporting structure) that fixes the outside of the synthase's head to keep it stationary as the shaft rotates inside of it, again similar to a rotary motor.

Simply put, an ADP that was once an ATP molecule (now having one less phosphate molecule because it's power has been used), is drawn along with a free phosphate molecule, into the space between two of the six molecular sections of the head. A bulge on the spinning camshaft like structure closes the space where the ADP molecule along with the free phosphate molecule are residing. This pressure presses the free phosphate molecule into contact with the ADP molecule and fuses them together to make a new ATP molecule. After a little more swirl of the shaft, the space reopens and the newly minted, charged-up-and-ready-to-go ATP molecule is released into the cell's matrix to go back to work. (Amazingly the head is spinning 100 times a second, non-stop)

For every turn of the shaft, three ADP molecules are converted back into new APT molecules and are put back into circulation as sources of energy to be used in all of the cell's energy-dependent functions. The energy is generated when the phosphate molecule is spilt away from the ATP: this is, without any exaggeration, the spark of life! This is the process that requires both food and air in animals and sunlight and water in plants.

Somehow this whole stunningly implausible process in the membranes of the mitochondria, along with the similar process of photosynthesis that takes place in chlorophyll, came into existence through a series, of as yet, unknown steps.

The discovery of the ATP synthase and all its unexpectedly bizarre structural complexity was revelatory for a number of scientists, as it should be. Once again, how in the world does something like this structure evolve in the traditional sense of the word? For many scientists, the structure and function of the ATP synthase is so extraordinary it enhanced their belief in the possibility of an underlying spiritual dynamic operating in the Universe. I would say this belief is not an unreasonable assumption to have, coupled with everything else we now know about this unlikely Universe of ours.

TWENTY

EUKARYOTIC CELLS AND MOTOR PROTEINS

As we have seen in a number of essays, the level of complexity that is now being revealed within cells is baffling. Just about everything is in manic-orchestrated motion, somewhat like a miniature city, with multifaceted supply chains in full swing. Fortunately, we can now go on Youtube and view high quality representations of these inner workings of cells that were unavailable and unimaginable just a few years ago.

A talented Australian named Drew Berry, for one, has done remarkable work at bringing this hidden world to life. The speed and the organization of the processes in play are mystifying to behold.

But with all such things we have to be in the right mindset to fully appreciate what we are looking at. It's easy for us to take this wild complexity for granted and not view it from the perspective of the probability of it ever having developed in the first place. How did all this come about from the simple laws of physics, and my catch phrase—scattered gas and dust floating in cold dark space?

Eukaryotic cells (cells with a nucleus) are where we come from, not only in distant time, but also in the merging of the sperm with the egg cell and their orchestrated development inside our mother's wombs. When this development of the embryo is viewed in depth, it's almost impossible to believe the level of sophistication that takes place in the growth of a fetus to get us ready to start meeting the demands of the world we will later encounter. That being said, let's take just one more small sample of the many extraordinary things going on inside of the cells in our bodies right now.

Of all the organelles and processes to be found inside our cells, one of the most improbable are the motor proteins that transmit vacuoles (bundles of cargo) along the micro-tubular infrastructure (suspension bridges) inside of our cells. I literally couldn't believe it when I first came across them. Incidentally, the tubular rod-like structures that the motor proteins travel along, like floating highways or bridges, are continually being constructed and disassembled in astonishing fashion.

The motor proteins, weirdly, look like Disney cartoon characters for all practical purposes. Again, I would encourage anyone to go to a Youtube video site and check them out. (You have to do this. They are truly that implausible. "The Inner Life of the Cell" is one of the best sites.) Imagine: they have two foot like appendages that look somewhat like the rounded block-like shoes of Pinocchio. Behind the shoe like configurations of molecules are two little legs that whirl around moving the motor proteins forward at a speed that is equivalent to around 60 miles an hour when brought up to our scale.

The legs are connected to a long, in comparison, rope like tangle of atoms that go up to the vacuoles which are orders of magnitude larger than the motor proteins (it's almost like an ant carrying a grape, size wise). At the end of the rope like tangle are different types of binding sites to transport hundreds of different types of cargos around the cell. The motor proteins go either way along the microtubules (different types go in different directions) directed by the electric charge at the end of the line. By some as-yet unknown fashion, they know what needs to be taken where and when. And when they get to their destination, they drop off their wide variety of freight (keep in mind, these are small collections of molecules doing all this). If another motor protein is on the same tube coming in the opposite direction, they can sense that too and move aside. They deposit their load (there are side ramps going off the larger micro-tubular structures that sometimes receive these loads) and then connect with another vacuole that needs to go somewhere else in the cell, which has one way or another been determined in advance.

It really doesn't make sense that any of this is actually true and is actually going on, but it is, in all your trillions of cells this very second.

In all the different types of motor proteins, the little leg-like appendages are powered by (you guessed it) ATP molecules that come into a binding site and then are broken apart, in the process releasing chemical energy (life's spark, which we talked about in the last essay). The ADP molecule floats out and winds up going through one of the millions of ATP synthases found in the cell's membranes, and the process is repeated over and over. By the way, the microtubules have alternating bands of different types of molecules with different electrical charges that the shoe-like structures latch onto and then let go of, to keep them moving along.

Eukaryotic cells are full of remarkable organelles and surprising processes that are starting to be understood and are utterly inexplicable in their complexity. We are starting to see our world now on a submicroscopic level that was totally unavailable just a few years ago. Once again, what were the odds of any of these things developing? The Earth would have been lucky just pulling off self-replicating RNA molecules let alone motor proteins and our next-door neighbor Fred!

TWENTY-ONE

HUMAN NATURE

Were there an Adam and Eve? Science surprisingly says yes, but with a couple of caveats. One is they never met (I'll try to explain shortly) and the other is that if there was anything even vaguely resembling the garden of Eden, it was somewhere in Africa or on an adjacent island.

Because of work that has been done in the analysis of the mutation rates of the markers found on the Y chromosome and the remnant DNA strands in the mitochondria, the sperm head doesn't contain mitochondria so it only comes through the mother's cells, the geneticists have weighed in and what they found caught just about everyone in the scientific community (interested in these things) off guard. Surprisingly, we all come from one father and one mother that were never acquainted in the Biblical sense (literally and figuratively). The science says they lived at least some thousand years apart (these numbers are in flux, but they were separated by thousands of years).

There are complicated reasons for this improbability, pertaining to the mutation rates of the two aforementioned markers found in cells that lead the scientists to make this determination. The woman (the figurative Eve) having lived about 150,000 years back (geneticists are continually refining these numbers), and the man (Adam) lived about 120,000 years ago. One of the reasons that have been put forth for why this was a possibility is that it was determined that a bottleneck probably took place in the human population about 70,000 years ago. This means only a relatively small group (a few thousand) of humans survived in some isolated area, and that within these people the markers that were mentioned were predominate.

What happened 70,000 years ago to create this result? A leading contender is the eruption of the Toba volcano in Indonesia that was catastrophic enough to bring our particular group of hominids to near extinction. There obviously could have been other reasons. It has been put forth that the pockets of humans at that time were already stressed for a variety of climatic reasons. But the fact remains that our remote ancestors were brought down to a population of just a few thousand at most, and this small group and their characteristics went on to explore and exploit the world.

An interesting aspect to this small population that once existed is that it led to the human race, as we know it, having less genetic diversity than a random sampling of groups of related chimps now found in West Africa, making humanity's general differences highly insignificant and superficial.

The so-called racial differences are primarily due to fairly recent environmental factors that humans met in their dispersal. One such adaptation is the ability to generate vitamin D in regions with less sunlight; this was done by a small genetic mutation that generated less melanin in the cells to lighten the skin of human populations in the north. This enabled people with this mutation to live successfully away from regions with less intense sunlight available. It also works in the opposite direction by darkening the skin, preventing the breakdown of a B vitamin if sunlight is too intense as in the more tropical latitudes. Both of these adaptations successfully prevented a wide range of detrimental physiological effects from developing over time.

It is interesting to note that the world that these people would start to move into out of Africa had at that time at least 4 other groups of hominid species. This led to confrontation and competition when the inevitable meetings of the two groups took place. The Neanderthals (with whom we share 99.5% of our genetic make-up) were in Europe at the time of our dispersal out of Africa and had been living there successfully for at least 400,000 years. When scientists compared our genomes to theirs recently, it was discovered that we have approximately 3 percent of their genes mixed in with ours (for a fairly obvious reason). This mixing and mingling, perhaps, took place in what is now the Middle East, thousands of years ago, where humans and Neanderthals had lived side-by-side for a long period of time, or perhaps in what is now Europe, when our kind of hominid invaded.

At the time when modern humans made their expansion out of Africa, another species of hominids (homoerectus) which had left Africa about 2 million years earlier were still dispersed throughout Asia. Along with them there was another "small" recently discovered splinter group of homoerectus (named playfully hobbits) that had ended up on the island of Flores in Indonesia; they had become dwarfed because of the limited resources on the island. This, by the way, is a common tendency with large animals when stuck on islands over long periods of time. (The skeletal remains of woolly mammoths the size of cows recently found on an isolated Siberian island being an example.)

Incidentally, wherever we went, if the early homoerectus populations had not put the animals on high alert, we made them pay the price by consuming them in large measure and in short order. The survival of the mega fauna in Africa was in large part because the animals knew we weren't to be trusted, because they had coevolved with us, or some other species akin to us. The animals that were acquainted with our type were leery and maintained their distance. The animals in Australia and North and South America, or any island we managed to land on didn't fare as well. They were easy pickings and we left a long series of mass extinctions in our wake, particularly the larger species we encountered. This is a brief picture of what science is telling us at this particular point in time; new findings will continue to come in and the hypothesis will change. New information is and should always be changing our perspective and the dates involved in our emergence. The best science is an open-ended pursuit of truth wherever it may lead.

So what are some of the attributes and characteristics that enabled us to spread so rapidly, dominating and eliminating most other large non-herding animals and any hominids still around, from such a small, almost-extinct founding population? We will consider a few human characteristics that seem to be of particular importance.

The first is we are a tribal-pack-like species with excellent communication skills and the ability to plan into the future (think of the tribal aspects of politics and religion). This planning ahead has to do with the development of our frontal lobes, the part of the brain that allows us to peer hypothetically into the future and to make up strategies to deal with it (this area of the brain develops slowly and is also where most of our socialization takes place). By the looks of it, the Neanderthals with their sloped back foreheads didn't have as much of this capacity as our ancestors had, even though they were tough as nails, as their skeletal remains seem to testify (a whole lot of broken bones, meaning they had a tendency to bring down large game the hard way—up close and personal). It took thousands of years but we put them out of business and claimed their hunting and living areas as our own (the unfortunate beginning of history as we know it!). The same went for any small remnant populations of homoerectus in Indonesia or elsewhere that we came across.

All this tribalism made us highly social and willing to make great sacrifices for the groups we belonged to (tribalism, nowadays pertains to whom we identify with for whatever reason). It also has, at times, the negative effect of making us prone to sacrifice common sense, as far as what we are willing to believe in, to be a part of a group. Studies indicate that we make decisions quite often unconsciously and emotionally before reason is employed. That is one of the reasons seemingly good people can have such diametrically opposing views on issues. They have made an emotional group-identity decision about what they believe and then their reasoning or rationalizations follow suit.

And along with that, the obvious fact that if some other person or group of people is considered a threat for legitimate or illegitimate reasons, all bets are off, and a shocking and appalling level of brutality is a distinct possibility (crack any history book for examples-look at our own civil war as a stark case in point). It is not hard to imagine that when different groups of people met up in prehistoric times, sometimes it didn't go very well. It is feasible the group that was the most aggressive, and had a strong and persuasive leader, along with a willingness to follow that leader's instructions, would usually carry the day. That group would inevitably transfer aspects of that aggressive nature on to future generations.

Our sports culture and our identifying with teams, along with their totem animals no less, are perhaps a reflection of those times and explains some of the despair we feel when our team loses the big game. When your tribe lost "the big game" in bygone days, it meant more than having another beer to try to forget about it. There was no moving on; you and your loved ones were vanquished or perhaps enslaved. These are just some of the many possible reverberations of our lingering tribalism, some good and some bad that can be recognized with only a little reflection. Our best qualities, such as altruism (making profound sacrifices for the group we belong to) and some of our conspicuously worst qualities (which we needn't get into) are a suggestion of those earlier times. We should keep all this in mind and try to put a check on some of our more negative base instincts when they start to get out of hand.

Another characteristic that can have explanatory power is our neotenistic tendencies; we seem to be a species that for some selective-pressure reason, we can assume, ended up retaining some of our juvenile characteristics into adulthood. Dogs are another species that have this quality; through our intervention and selective breeding dogs are neotenous wolves. They remain playful (as we do) as they grow older and have a tendency to need and enjoy parental figures (as we do), and also never lose that child-like (puppy) love for us that is so endearing. For many of us they are obviously like our children. Of course, that same type of tendency is both, again, good and bad. Good when we rally around our father or mother figures, to defend our nation for a just cause. Bad when sometimes the cause is unjust and we blindly follow orders that are later regretted. Everyone has a mind full of these types of examples they can consider. But mostly I think these neotenous tendencies are a real plus for humanity and lead to many of life's enjoyments.

It is interesting to look at a picture of a baby chimp; they look markedly human with their high foreheads. Then look at an adult chimp, they look markedly Neanderthal. Maybe we out-competed Neanderthals because of our developed frontal lobes as earlier mentioned, along with our neotenous tendencies.

As a quick aside, much to my exasperation, I read recently that domesticated animals like sheep and cows have lost brain mass (about 10%) because they don't really have to survive by using their wits anymore, and that we domesticated humans are starting to fall into that category or perhaps are already in it (just an idle thought in my shrinking brain).

Another characteristic that is more physical than psychological is our orientation toward aquatic environments that most other primates don't have. Maybe we ended up bottlenecked on an island and we had to exploit the surrounding oceans and rivers, heading into them for our survival. We have a number of physiological indications that suggest that might have been the case.

We have only a little hair (which is an aquatic adaptation in mammals). Think of the other primates like apes, chimps and baboons; they remain covered in hair. We also have a subcutaneous layer of fat (a marine adaptation that was a leading cause for the theory to develop in the first place, when it was noticed to be a human characteristic). We also have a nose sheath to prevent water from entering when we dive or swim. Our eyes tear up, and those tears are high in salt (other primates simply don't shed tears, but crocodiles do). We excrete a lot of salt and water for that matter in other ways, and you would have to assume that salt and water weren't in short supply when we developed those traits. We additionally have a dive reflex which slows our metabolism when we are submerged in water. (Splashing water on our faces to calm ourselves perhaps reflects back to this reflex.)

Have you seen, perhaps, the pictures of babies that enjoy being in and under water shortly after birth? The list of "semi-aquatic" adaptations goes on with many more things to add to the list to be considered. This hypothesis is gradually gaining some acceptance. (I obviously like it.)

One last thing, if we didn't have aquatic adaptations would there be any swim events in the Olympics? Would "Planet of Apes" chimps have swim events in their games if they had them? Probably not!

Anyway, a lot of our psychological and physiological characteristics (not all of them of course) can be explained at least partially through looking at us as a tribal, neotenistic, domesticated (you, not me) aquatically oriented species of primates, with, of course, underlying spiritual tendencies.

TWENTY-TWO

EMERGENCE AND EVOLUTION

We have seen in this series of essays one remarkable characteristic after another become manifest in the Universe's unfolding. The Universe starts with a point of space, time and energy that lacks any distinguishing qualities other than unimaginable heat. Yet almost instantly, things start to emerge; they aren't evolving in the typical sense of the word, because there is no adaptive competition in what was springing into existence. It all had to have been there on some intrinsic level already, but in a latent pre existing aspect of space that would only be revealed over time. The underlying premise of these essays is that It's beyond a reasonable doubt that this, what we are experiencing right now, is not some sort of lucky happenstance and that we are just fortunate byproducts of a long series of incredibly fine-tuned physical properties inherent in this Universe of ours, with all of these properties springing into existence spontaneously, for no apparent reason. From what we have learned in our scientific investigation, that seems highly improbable.

It seems more reasonable and likely that there is a guiding and sustaining force that created the conditions necessary to move things forward in the direction of the complexity that culminates in life and consciousness. This seems more probable than just blind chance at work generating the Universe and all the forces and forms necessary for us to be here.

To get to higher levels of complexity, there has to be initial material and processes in place, in order to allow higher complexity to develop when conditions permit. This has been evident all the way up the line, starting with quarks and ending up with self-conscious beings, like us. This is not to deny evolution at all, but to see evolution as a process that takes place when there are life forms with a genetic code that can be acted upon by environmental and selective pressures. It is just that if we look close enough, we run into many things along the way, leading to the complexity we experience, that would be virtually unachievable if they didn't exist as hidden latent potentialities waiting for their time to be expressed.

As I have mentioned previously, the Infinite that brought the Universe into existence logically couldn't have found anything outside of Itself with which to make it. And whatever name it is given, it must be infinite and eternal and possess an imaginative-creative power that is inconceivable to us. We can only get a glimpse of it as it is revealed and reflected within ourselves and in our Universe at large.

In our Western Civilization, which has been dominated until fairly recently by a Biblical historical perspective, we have had this ongoing conflict of science versus a literal interpretation of the Bible. I firmly believe it doesn't have to be that way. For instance, in the higher modes of Eastern thought, because the scriptures are considered to be more metaphorical and not literal by and large, there hasn't been generated the same level of hostility and rancor that we are so used to between science and religion in the West. The Universe from their perspective is a creative expression of the Infinite, generating a tendency for them to feel more like participants and less like lords of dominance, as is quite often the case with us in the West. Some of us go as far as to consider the world as having been made specifically for us, with a God up there and Nature being perceived and felt as distinct from us. This perspective seems to give us the right and license to use and abuse our planet as we await the end of times.

That being said, whatever our underlying point of view, we can, without much of a stretch, view our existence as something wildly improbable, and enjoy it as such. As they say, we are stardust, and the unlikely magic we experience as consciousness is perhaps, as many believe, an interface with Spirit that can be experienced in its fullness when we settle into ourselves in calm contemplation.

TWENTY-THREE

IT'S HARD TO BELIEVE!

If the nucleus of an atom was brought up to the size of an orange and placed in the middle of a football field, it would not have its first electron evident until the outer edge of the stadium.

If all the space were to be taken out of the atoms that comprise humanity, the entire human race (all 7 billion or so of us) would fit into the space of a sugar cube. (Remember sugar cubes?)

Within the infolded membranes of the mitochondria in our bodies, every second the quadrillion (many zeros) ATP synthases generate more ATP molecules than the number of stars in our galaxy (well over a 100 billion).

And if the mitochondria membranes in our bodies containing the ATP synthases were laid out flat, they would cover 4 football or soccer fields.

Things are moving incredibly fast sub-atomically; everything is in perpetual motion. In a finger snap, one of your molecules in that finger that was snapped has vibrated 10 billion times. For each one of those vibrations, the electrons have whirled around the nucleus of an atom in that molecule about 1 million times. And for each one of those electron orbits, the protons and neutrons in the nucleus have spun around another million times. And what about the quarks? You guessed it. In the protons and neutrons of the aforementioned atom, the quarks within them will have whirled around, again, about a million times. (These facts were taken, as a number of the others here, from Mark Whittle's excellent course on cosmology, part of the Teaching Companies' Great Courses curriculum.)

If the mass of the average adult male or female were converted into energy, it would be enough to power the electrical needs of the entire United States for about 30 years. (And you need a nap!)

If you took that mass of yours on a jet plane to Miami and instead just kept on going, you would reach the "nearest" star in just under 5 million years (just in time for lunch!)

The amount of neurons in your brain, rapidly firing away, hopefully, is about coincidentally the same amount as the stars in our galaxy (remember, around 100 billion).

100 billion is a lot. How can we imagine it? There are roughly between 100 to 300 billion stars in our Milky Way galaxy. On a clear night in the desert, you can see perhaps 2,000 or so. If you make a square box with the sides about a yard high and a yard wide and put a very small pile of salt in your palm and throw it in, this is around the amount of stars you see in the night sky. If you fill the box up with salt, this is about 100 billion grains of salt: the amount of stars in our galaxy. And in just the visible Universe, there are about the same number of Galaxies. (You will remember that because of the lack of curvature found in space, what we can see is a small fraction of what actually exists.)

If the earth's orbit were shrunk to the size of the head of a ballpoint pen, then our Galaxy would be proportionally the size of the United States. And if you imagined our Galaxy being the relative size of the infield at some baseball park in the middle of the country, then the observable Universe would proportionately be again about the size of the United States. Always remember, all this was at one time not even as big as the head of that previously mentioned ballpoint pen.

How fast are we moving through space right now? Think about it for a moment and guess, and then we'll do the math.

Earth's rotational speed: 1,000 mph (miles per hour)

Earth's orbital speed: 66,667 mph (exact isn't it?)

Sun moving through space (within the galaxy, its movement is upward and also a little sideways): 60,000 mph

Our spinning Milky Way galaxy is rotating at a leisurely 550,000 mph.

The movement of our galaxy toward its inevitable collision with the Andromeda galaxy: 252,000 mph.

And what about the movement of the local group of galaxies we are a part of, you might ask, well it is 2,237,000 mph.

That's about it, unless you're traveling in a car or train as you read this. You can add that on if you like.

So how fast are we moving through space at this moment? You probably guessed it: 2,855,000 mph.

A look at deep time: let's take a quick imaginary journey back in time with a millennium (1000 years) being a second.

2 seconds-the birth of Christ.

10 seconds-the birth of agriculture.

30 seconds-Cro-Magnon men and perhaps women are cave painting in what is now southern France.

18 hours – the dinosaurs became extinct after a large meteorite impact in the now named Yucatan Peninsula in Central America.

4 ½ days – the Cambrian explosion of multicellular life leading to all the known life forms. For the previous 40 days life has been just single cells, with a few living in colonies.

44 days – life mysteriously comes into existence.

53 days – the earth is formed out of gas and dust in cold dark space.

150 days – The Universe comes forth in an explosion of time, energy and space that is much smaller than this period.

Before that—Infinite Spirit.

TWENTY-FOUR

WHAT DIFFERENCE DOES IT MAKE?

Does this perspective that we have been exploring make any difference? Perhaps it can if we take it to heart. Here are a number of things it can possibly affect.

When we consider ourselves to be embedded in a Universe with an underlying Spiritual aspect or dynamic to it, we can see ourselves as being co-creators and active participants in our limited way.

Also it has often been the experience of those holding this perspective that help on many different levels and in many different ways, is often forthcoming when it is needed.

From a psychological point of view, trying to enhance our life experience by some form of spiritual introspection or meditation into deeper levels of our minds and consciousness can lead to greater personality integration; because we cannot suppress as much, we end up processing and dealing with things that need to be dealt with. And the more honestly and effectively we address our issues, the better we can move forward with our lives in a more positive way.

As we open ourselves up to the Spirit within and without, we slow ourselves down, and our timing inevitably becomes better. Things are more likely to fall into place without our anxiously pushing forward on something that will, out of necessity, just take time.

Also, because we are more open and feel Spirit to be a positive underlying aspect of our consciousness, insight, answers to questions, and creative inspiration come more readily.

Occurrences, which can be called mundane miracles, start taking place. Things happen that are really quite extraordinary; coincidences that seem to be beyond luck happen more frequently. Fortunate events start coming our way more often. And the inevitable bad situations that arise in our lives are more effectively faced and resolved.

And it's hard not to become more appreciative and grateful. (A lot of work goes into making and sustaining this unnecessary Universe of ours we can safely assume.)

If we believe that the Universe is a Spiritual manifestation, we realize that it is all a miracle, and because of that fact, it is not too far-fetched to believe that other aspects of reality could possibly exist. Maybe there really are other dimensions where passed-on loved ones reside and our destinies await us. Other dimensions and spiritual possibilities are not to be totally dismissed from what we have seen in this unlikely Universe of ours. The Infinite by its very nature knows no limits.

A friend once remarked to me that it was all so confusing and complicated and he wasn't sure exactly how to deal with it all, and was confused as to what he should do. I mentioned to him that it really doesn't have to be that complicated, at least from a spiritual perspective. Just do your best with what life brings your way. Try to find something meaningful to do, and set and follow through on worthwhile goals. Also, as we have always been told, follow the golden rule and treat others the way you would like to be treated yourself (with a little respect, consideration and kindness) and try to love your neighbor, or at least try to like them a little (even Fred!). And, of course, try to commune with the Infinite Spirit through Nature or some form of meditation—for that is a very good thing to do.

Printed in the United States
By Bookmasters